Vincent Crapanzano

The Fifth World of Forster Bennett

PORTRAIT OF A NAVAJO

Foreword to the Bison Books Edition by the author

UNIVERSITY OF NEBRASKA PRESS
LINCOLN AND LONDON

Library of Congress Cataloging-in-Publication Data
Crapanzano, Vincent, 1939–
The fifth world of Forster Bennett; portrait of a Navajo / Vincent
Crapanzano.—Bison Books ed. / foreword to the Bison Books
edition by the author.
p. cm.
Originally published: New York: Viking Press, 1972.
Includes bibliographical references.
ISBN 0-8032-6431-3 (pbk.: alk. paper)
1. Bennett, Forster.   2. Navajo Indians—Biography.   I. Title.
E99.N3.B463   2003
979.1004'972—dc21   2002075093

VINCENT CRAPANZANO

Foreword to the Bison Books Edition

Reading *The Fifth World of Forster Bennett* for the first time in more than twenty years, perhaps longer, I was overcome not only by how much time had passed since that summer on the Navajo reservation but by how much of it I "mis-remembered" and how much more I had forgotten. Maurice Blanchot once said that an author can never read his or her own work the way others do. Though Blanchot's observation is drawn from a complex philosophy, edged always by death and non-being, it can be taken—at least I'm willing to take it—on a much simpler level. When reading his own writing an author will never have the distance or perspective his readers have. That seems obvious enough. What is not so obvious is that every word, every event described—indeed, the evoked events, however they were experienced, as fact or fantasy, as remembered or constructed—gives rise to prepossessive memories, most of which hover indeterminately between recall and forgetting. With the passage of time, as I discovered while rereading *The Fifth World* after all these years, the forgetting comes to dominate understanding and, as it does, an author's reading of what he has written comes closer to a stranger's take on it; that is, the text read anew becomes a persistent reminder of the travesty of his own memory. With the failure of memory and the fading of forgetfulness, an author's work—at least *The Fifth World*, for me—becomes a sort of allegory, elegiac in tone, a *vanitas*, an intimation not of immortality, as Wordsworth famously put it, but of mortality.

The allegory of death I am describing could easily be translated into an allegory of the fate of the Indian, but to do so
would be almost obscene. I don't need to rehearse the disap-
pearance of entire cultures, the mutilation of the ones that
survived, or the relegation of the survivors themselves to the
margins of a society that is unwilling to acknowledge its own
brutality, even as it flatters itself with stipulated goodness and
innocence. I refuse, in the event, to stress "the death of the
Indian," if only because those Native Americans who have survived, however sadly, have survived despite all this. For that
they must be applauded.

As I wrote at the time, though arguably in different words,
my aim was not to indulge sixties' Americans with yet another
story of Indian chiefs, shamans, and idealizations of one Indian culture or another, but rather to call their attention to
the fact that many Native Americans, like the Navajos I came
to know, were living in abject conditions without succumbing
to the abjection imposed on them. There were, to be sure,
exceptions, such as the proverbial "Indian drunks" whom many
Anglos prefer to understand in terms of the Indians' suscep-
tibility to alcohol rather than as the result of the undermining
conditions forced upon them. Of course, those conditions are
often enough taken as the product of an essentially defective
Indian culture (as if there was only one such culture) that has
resisted positive change by, among other things, failing to encourage its members to pull themselves up, in "the American
way," by their bootstraps. Such chains of eschewal of responsibility, devoid of historical grasp, ignore the possibility of the lack of
possibility—of the lack of bootstraps to begin with.

As I turned my field notes into a book, I thought naively
that I could accomplish something by writing about reservation life. I miss that level of ambition. But today I recognize
more than I did then that the conditions in which the Navajos
found themselves were not altogether unique. Not only were
there other Native Americans living in similar conditions, there
were—there are—other groups, most notably the rural poor
of all backgrounds, who live abjectly in a land of abjection
which they, or at least some of them, still believe is a land of

promise. Compared to many of these people, the Navajos, like other Native Americans, have an advantage. However mutilated their culture may have been, however much of it they may have "lost," that culture, their traditions, embedded as they are in their landscape, their memory, their thoughts and actions, are still a resonant reference point and give them an identity that many other rural peoples simply do not have. With this possibility of cultural orientation and identity, and with extraordinary will, Navajos have overcome much and been able to celebrate themselves, their traditions, and, above all, their accomplishments. In making this observation I'm not suggesting that all's well or soon will be well on the reservation. This is certainly not the case. (Only a decade ago, 56 percent of all the Navajos living on the reservation were living below the poverty level. Their average annual income was $4,106, as compared to the overall U.S. average of $19,082.) Like other marginalized peoples, many Native Americans have succumbed to that debilitating status of "victim," a phenomenon that becomes more and more prevalent as the society at large—and the government, certainly—becomes less and less generous.

The Navajos are a subtle people, something I've come to appreciate more over the years. Often, through indirection and sometimes even silence, they convey far more than the more verbose among us. During the summer I spent with the people of Little Bluff, they conveyed their suspicions of me, sometimes directly (as when they told me that I would go back East and write a book that would make a lot of money), but more often indirectly, through exquisitely timed, almost minimalist innuendo. During my first days in Little Bluff I was told several times about a white man, "an anthropologist," they sometimes said—he was, in fact, an internationally known psychologist—who had asked them to describe what they'd seen in the pictures he had shown them (presumably Thematic Apperception Tests), and then, after paying them a pittance, had walked away without bothering to ease the anxiety they had experienced or even address their curiosity about his research. They had felt violated; they were violated. They knew something had been taken from them, to be used in ways they couldn't understand, as so much else had been taken from them over the centuries. I asked Forster about this psychologist, but he had little to say. As the summer progressed, though, he would mention the man from time to time. Then, one day, he told me about another man, a drifter who had spent a winter in Little Bluff and then had raped and murdered a neighbor's daughter. It was only later that I came to realize the extent to which Forster, and other people of Little Bluff who mentioned the drifter, were revealing their fear of me, their suspicion, and how, by revealing it, they were—I have to believe this—beginning to trust me.

This revelation—it was a warning as well—kept intruding as I reread *The Fifth World*, and, maybe because of it, I kept wanting to change what I had written. I was embarrassed by the way I had referred to the Navajos as Indians (not to mention how I had called the anthropologists "men"). The word "Indian," though current then, seems disrespectful in today's politically charged climate. But, more important, I was embarrassed by how many of my generalizations seemed to verge on precisely the stereotypy that I had tried to avoid by writing a journal about particular people and by relying on the presumption—which I justified, when I bothered thinking about it at all, by my understanding of anthropology and its scientific privilege—that allowed me to intrude so insistently into the lives of Forster Bennett and his family and friends. I think particularly of the way I somehow felt entitled to sneak into Forster's room when he was out of the house to take an inventory of his things. At the time I was perhaps less sensitive than some of my colleagues, but my presumption did, I believe, reflect a stance that was all too prevalent at the time.

As anthropologists we must, I suppose, recognize that our research is not altogether different from that of the journalist and the detective. We are there to discover something, whether it be a story or data that we somehow find significant. We justify a great many practices that we know are, on some level, suspect, and we do it on the basis of this "significance." We may or may not be justified, but we have also to remember that our research is not really very different from what all of us do when we set about to discover the details of something interesting that has happened, to make sense of it, and to represent it. The people we work with are often, though not always, seduced by our presence, and they may even enjoy talking to us. Many people in Little Bluff certainly liked talking to me, and they certainly enjoyed pulling my leg with their stories. Perhaps it was their own kind of revenge.

What I ended up portraying is not necessarily what the people of Little Bluff would want to have had portrayed. No one likes being objectified. No one likes becoming a figure in someone else's story, someone else's argument. No one likes to have his privacy exposed, even if he remains masked in the exposure. When I wrote *The Fifth World* I was perhaps less conscious than I ought to have been of the embarrassment the book could cause. I took refuge in those maskings of identity but, even so, I knew I was addressing real people who might read what I'd written. I also knew, or at least presumed to know, that by calling attention to the everyday life of the people of Little Bluff, and by doing it without distancing myself from what I had to say, I was giving those people a respect that is often, and easily, lost in more protective ethnographies. All of us who engage in ethnographic research—and I include informants as well as anthropologists here—have to submit to a rigorous realism. This is not to say that each of us will understand or value "realism" in the same way. We will not. And that is precisely the asymmetry we must realistically acknowledge.

By casting myself in as realistic and not always as flattering a fashion as I could have in my portrayal of Little Bluff, I must have eased my own burden of responsibility, perhaps even guilt. In other words, I embraced (as I am now embracing, in a sense) that confessional rhetoric, so prevalent in the United States, that often appeases our moral disquiet through personal revelation. I still stand by the importance of the "I" in social scientific research and description, but today I would focus on the dialogical relationship, in fact and in fantasy, that constitutes the "I" as it is constituted by the "you," and on the discursive constraints that govern that relationship. The

I—the several I's—in *The Fifth World* have to be seen, at least in part, as a response to my Navajo interlocutors, particularly Forster Bennett. But they must also be understood as a response to my interlocutors back home—my professors, members of my family, a lover, and everything that those people represented for me. There can be no purity of response. What I would stress today is the degree to which I (with Forster and other Navajos) was able to manipulate the genres of research and description, which are far less constraining in transcultural and therefore exceptional research than those that govern our everyday lives.

Reactions to *The Fifth World*, when it was first published, were either very positive or dismissive. In general the popular press was positive, while responses I received from some of my anthropological colleagues were quite negative. Some insisted that what I had written wasn't "anthropology," as if that mattered. I never claimed it was or wasn't anthropology. I found, and still find, that such classifications represent the worst of academic territorialism. I have never assumed that a book written by an anthropologist is by definition "anthropological" any more than a book written by a poet is poetry. The anthropologist, like every other writer, is confronted with a task: to convey, as best as he or she can, what she or he has learned and thinks worthy of communicating. How one conveys these "significant findings" is a question of craft. To reduce what one "finds" in the field into stipulated genres or prevalent theoretical constructs is to translate "difference" into the "conventionally different" and thereby lose that *difference*, that particularity of experience, its truth, and (it is hoped) the creative disquiet it produces.

Some of my anthropology critics seemed less concerned with my possible misrepresentations of the Navajos than they were with my misrepresentations of anthropological research per se. They were distressed by my revelation of what they took to be anthropology's backstage. They wanted to preserve the discipline's purity. I do not claim that what I revealed—as a student struggling to accommodate what I had learned in the classroom about anthropological methods to the experi-

ence of actually living in Little Bluff—exemplified anthropological fieldwork. I am not sure that one can, in fact, charac-
terize fieldwork other than to say that it involves intense self-
reflective observations of a people—that is, their practices and
beliefs—who are constituted, heuristically, as different. I do
know that to deny the underside of that practice is to facili-
tate its intrusion into one's findings and into the representation of those findings. A sense of failure is inherent in all
anthropological research, if for no other reason than that
anthropologists, as stipulated outsiders, can never gain full
entry into the lives of the people they study. This sense of
failure, of incompletion (at best), becomes a sort of govern-
ing secret that, like the loneliness of the outsider, lies behind
all anthropological accounts.

Some of the Navajos who read *The Fifth World* liked it. Others were silent. Still others said I was "right" to describe what
the Anglos had done to them. Several Hopis said the book
was just like "the Navies." For me the most moving review came
from a Native American writer from the Northwest Coast who
said that although he had never been on the Navajo reservation, what I had written reminded him of his own reservation
life. He wrote that what I'd described had needed to be said.
In rereading *The Fifth World* I noted how often the Navajos,
particularly the young Navajos who had been to school, referred to *the Navajos* in stereotypic and at times belittling terms.
They often made use of the "they," as when Bill Thomas repeated several times that the Navajos in Little Bluff—"they"—
"didn't get the concept." (He was referring to the introduction of new agricultural methods.) Or when Mr. Grant complained that "the people" didn't understand that they would
have to pay for the water that came from the main line. In
each of these cases the Navajos seemed to have been deper-
sonalized and judged the way Anglos—as Anglos were understood—might have judged them. I know that what I have written, if it is read by the Navajos, might seem to support that
"outside" vantage point and encourage self-deprecation and
alienation. I hope it also will reveal to my Navajo readers the
way that stance functioned some thirty years ago.

My experience with the Navajos, certainly with Forster Bennett, has impressed itself on my biography. I often thought about Forster, though I never saw him again. He died more than fifteen years ago. I should note that my experience on the reservation, and I am sure Forster's experience of my visit, were tarnished by the machinations of an embittered anthropologist who had fled the East, which he declared decadent, for a world out West among the "Indians." It was a world in which he indulged himself, though by definition it always remained out of his own reach. I considered Forster my friend, and I knew he considered me his friend. I was proud of my book—it was my first—and I wanted to surprise him with it and to share whatever earnings I had with him. The surprise was precluded—and with that preclusion a separation was created. Forster accepted, with a realism our encounter demanded, much of what I had to say, though he must have been embarrassed and may even have felt betrayed. He never allowed it, I believe, to poison our relationship.

When Gary Dunham at the University of Nebraska Press asked me if his organization could republish *The Fifth World*, I was editing a section of my latest book, *Imaginative Horizons*, on the Navajo world-view. I have always been an admirer of that world-view—of its insistence on the incipient, on the creative power of the word, and on the harmony of the universe. The Navajos recognize the obligation that such an outlook puts on them, indeed on all human beings, to preserve that harmony and restore it when it has been destroyed. It stresses the flowering of the world—a process, always in motion—from within, from a center that resists final denomination but which they identify, if I understand them correctly, with their land, their homeland, the *diné bikéyah*, as well as with their hearts. After "things" had been placed on earth, First Man and First Woman, those descriptively illusive first human beings, plucked a feather from a bald eagle and blew on it, saying, "From now on everything is on the move. Nothing will be still, not even the water, not even the rock." By constituting a historical moment *The Fifth World* defies that view, that movement, as it marks the changes, the movement, that have come afterward—continual incipience.

FOREWORD

The Fifth World of Forster Bennett was written several years ago when I was still a graduate student of anthropology. It touches upon material dear to the anthropologist and even deals, in part, with the role of the anthropologist, but it is not, at least in any technical sense, a work of anthropology and was never meant to be one—despite the fact that readers who insist on classifying a work not in its own terms but by whatever particular label society attaches to its author will inevitably judge it as such.

The Fifth World is, rather, a personal account of the reactions—sometimes naïve, often arrogant—of an "Anglo," an East-Coaster who had been oriented more toward Europe than toward his own country, during one short summer on the Navaho reservation. Although it may reveal more of him than of the Navaho—and this is perhaps as it should be—it does attempt to portray something of the life of the everyday Navahos, who are manifestly not everyday persons despite the categorizing and theorizing, the speculating and projecting, the analyzing of the observer who is the "I" of the book.

It is this "I" who may offend the social scientist. It is this "I" who, to borrow from Irving Goffman, brings backstage front—always embarrassing to actors who are discovered out of role. It is this "I" who so seldom appears in the literature of the social sciences, despite the frequent use of the first person singular. It is this "I" who enables me, writer-turned-reader, to discover something more in this journal than I had known to be there. And it is this "I" who has prevented me from dressing up the manuscript in the years that have gone by since the book was written.

The "I" of the book, a graduate student in the social sciences, was determined to learn about the Navaho people, the *Diné,* and had to keep reminding himself, and may have even forgotten for a time, that the Navaho were people more like himself than different but different nevertheless. He had to learn that the reservation, like the ghettos of other "culturally classified inferiors"—and there are still a great many for white middle-class society —could be a tempting stage on which to play out those most unflattering impulses that lie within the black murk of the unconscious, to use Freud's expression.

The Fifth World has had a long and difficult history, which would surely have prevented me from seeking its final publication had it not reconfirmed the lesson of that summer—the lesson of the ease and obliviousness and even callousness with which the Indian can be, and constantly is being, dehumanized, whether in the name of science or through gestures of assistance and so-called charity. I did it, often enough, in scientific curiosity. Others—this is probably more frequent today—do it out of a desire, a "responsibility," to help. Today's secular missionaries are often as incapable of self-scrutiny as their proselytizing nineteenth-century counterparts. They too can be psychological parasites who must render their hosts inhuman, inanimate even, before they can gorge themselves on acts of compassion.

And the Indian has been host to these beneficent parasites, who have fed on him as they have fed on the blacks, the chicanos, and the "primitives," "preliterates," and "traditionalists" of Africa, New Guinea, and Southeast Asia; and, as such, he has become precisely what he should not be: a fringe citizen, a marginal man, a member of a minority group to be studied and helped, to be assimilated even.

I am reminded of one of these secular missionaries, one of these students—fortunately they are not all like him—who went so far as to marry an Indian, not a Navaho but an Indian from another reservation in another part of the country. He called me out one evening to look at a particularly beautiful sunset. I had been talking to his wife, whom he hadn't bothered to call out but who trailed along after me. He pretentiously compared the color of the sunset to a stained-glass window in a rather obscure cathedral in France. I said nothing. His wife asked him why he couldn't look, simply, at the sunset without having to compare it to some man-made creation. I was moved. I had been taken in by the comparison. But he, the student, the altruist, the assimilationist, could only snap, "What would you know about these things?"

Another reservation. Another time. But it could have happened on the Navaho reservation as well.

And I must not forget her, his Indian wife. She walked silently back to the house and never saw the sun set.

THE FIFTH WORLD OF
FORSTER BENNETT

INTRODUCTION

THE NAVAHO TELL OF FOUR WORLDS through which their primordial ancestors progressed. These worlds are hemispheres, stacked one on another, each supported by pillars of precious stone, and each lit with color—red, blue, yellow, and black and white—rather than light. As the ancestors of the Navaho moved up from world to world, driven by sorcery and witchcraft, they developed social and cultural institutions. When they finally emerged into the fifth, or present, world, First Man and First Woman created the sun and the moon, and light came to predominate. It is this world which is generally recognized as the best.

Today the Navaho inhabit the largest Indian reservation in the United States: some twenty-four thousand square miles of what is often euphemistically called semiarid land, in Arizona, New Mexico, and Utah. Although

Navaho mythology and legend are filled with stories of the early inhabitants of this fifth world, historically little is known of the origin of the People, as the Navaho call themselves. Linguistic evidence suggests a northern origin, for they, like their cousins the Apache, speak a tongue which is closely related to the Athabaskan languages spoken by certain Indian tribes in the interior of northwestern Canada. No date can be set with any certainty for the Navaho's arrival in the Southwest. Some authorities believe that they may have entered the area as early as the eleventh century, but archeological and linguistic (lexico-statistical) analysis suggests a somewhat later date. Their migration was probably completed about six hundred years ago. It is not unreasonable to assume that these early hunters and gatherers borrowed cultural practices from the Plains Indians as they moved south across western Canada and the United States, but the People owe their greatest debt to the sophisticated Pueblo villagers who already inhabited the Southwest when the Navaho arrived. It was the Pueblo who taught them weaving and agricultural techniques and who inspired them to elaborate their ceremonial system and religious lore.

By the seventeenth century, according to Franciscan missionaries in the area, the Navaho were already agriculturists who probably supplemented their economy by hunting, gathering edible plants, and raiding their Pueblo neighbors. It was from these raids that the Navaho obtained their first sheep and horses, which had been introduced into the area by the Spanish in the sixteenth century and which were to revolutionize Navaho social and economic organization. From then until 1846, when the United States took possession of northwestern Mexico, Navaho history was characterized by constant warfare. As-

similation of Pueblo ways continued,* and there was some
contact with European culture, especially by those Navahos who were taken as slaves.

The first years of the American occupation were rela-
tively peaceful, but by 1860 all peace had deteriorated. In
1862 the Navaho took advantage of the army's preoccupa-
tion with the Civil War and increased their raids. By
June of the following year the situation was considered so
grave that Colonel Kit Carson was given a free hand to
round up the Navaho. This he accomplished by starving
out the people through a systematic destruction of all
their crops and livestock. The Navaho were then marched
some three hundred miles to Fort Sumner, near Santa Fe,
where the 8,500 men, women, and children lived miserably
for four years. In 1868 the federal government finally recognized the failure of the Fort Sumner experiment, sent
the Navaho back to their land, and provided them with
three and a half million acres—a fraction of their former
area—and thirty-five thousand sheep and goats. Although
the Navaho population, which is one of the most rapidly
expanding populations on earth, is now at least fourteen
or fifteen times as large as in its Fort Sumner days, tribal
land has been increased only fourfold over the years—the
reservation is today about the size of West Virginia. Recent estimates of the population have been as high as
140,000. Already by 1930 the land base could not support
the population. The federal government was forced to in-
troduce an arbitrary program of stock reduction and strict

* Of the Pueblo the Hopi are today perhaps in closest contact with
the Navaho. Their villages actually form an enclave within the
larger Navaho reservation. Yet, despite this physical proximity,
there is surprisingly little mixing between the two peoples. Their
differences are given symbolic expression in land disputes, some of
which have been taken as far as the United States Supreme Court.

grazing restrictions. Many rich Navahos suddenly found themselves with only a fraction of their former holdings. The results of this program, like the results of other Navaho public works projects of the thirties, were disappointing in terms of the resources expended, and they produced a mistrust and resentment of the government which has by no means disappeared.

Although I was assured that conditions had improved dramatically over the last few decades—and indeed there were many signs on the reservation that they had—the summer I spent there left me discouraged. The Navaho problem seemed nearly insoluble to me then. A large percentage of the Navaho were living at a low subsistence level, eking a tiny living from the land or apathetically awaiting a monthly welfare check. Efforts at education, and even forced relocation, have done little to ease population pressures. The traditional Navaho response to population pressure—migration and territorial expansion (an issue which is still alive in the federal courts in the Navaho-Hopi land disputes)—is of course no longer satisfactory. Most specialists who have considered the problem have looked to Navaho cultural patterns and psychological make-up for an explanation of why the people insist on remaining on the reservation, but consideration should probably also be given to America's Indian policy and to the opportunities offered the Navaho in the overall American social scene. Arbitrary and inconsistent federal policy has often left the Navaho with little choice but to retreat stoically into himself and his family, to seek solace in "the old people's way" or evangelical practices, or to escape through liquor or millenarian dreams. Even a superficial examination of Navaho school curricula during the last fifty years, for example, will point to this sort of vacillation in federal policy. A child who in one year is taught

only "white man's subjects," with the consequent dis-
missal, if not denigration, of his own tradition, is encouraged the following year to study, admire, and participate
in Navaho ways. Opportunities for the people off-reservation are poor. The Navaho, like other Indians, have come
in contact largely with "marginal Americans" and are, as
George Devereux noted about the Plains Indians, acculturated into marginal American society. They end up living in a sort of no man's land which places great pressures
upon them and offers them little comfort. The inherent
limitations of such a social position may be tolerable to
some Navahos but certainly not to the majority. A few
Navahos have tended to identify almost completely with
the white man's world; others, mostly older, with the traditional but moribund Navaho world; and the vast majority tend to vacillate between the two. Reporters who come
in contact with the most acculturated Navaho in circumstances that would force even the more ambivalent Indian
to be his most "American" often leave with an
oversimplified version of Indian life and problems within
the larger American context.

Little Bluff, where most of the events recorded in this
journal took place, can best be conceived of as a theater of
social change in which the "Americanization" of a Navaho
population is being played out. As in all such dramas, cultural conflict is the leitmotif. The Navaho of Little Bluff
are torn between the ways of the old people and the ways
of the Anglo as they picture him. Unlike their Pueblo
neighbors, the Navaho have tended to respond individu-
ally to the pressures of acculturation. It is not unusual to
observe startling contrasts in adjustment and adaptation
even among brothers and sisters of similar age. This indi-
vidualism has its roots deep in Navaho cultural tradition.
Traditional Navaho social organization can be seen as a

response to the demands imposed by sheepherding in a semi-arid land. The basic social unit was the nuclear family, consisting of husband, wife (or wives), and unmarried children, who moved from one isolated camp to another in accordance with the grazing demands of their herds. Each campsite consisted of a six-sided, one-room hut of mud, logs, and grass, called a hogan, and a brush arbor in which, when weather permitted, most of the daily work took place. This closed-in, isolated sort of living arrangement tended to promote a good deal of emotional inbreeding, which was often deflected outward, as Clyde Kluckhohn has noted, in the form of witchcraft accusations.

Although the camps were isolated, other members of the wife's family—the Navaho are matrilocal—lived in neighboring camps and cooperated in economic, ceremonial, and other activities. Work or ritual requiring still wider participation followed clan lines but was delimited by geographical considerations, since the members of each of the fifty-odd Navaho clans were not concentrated in a single area. Clan membership followed the mother's line (matriliny) and served primarily to regulate marriage. Marriage to a member of one's own clan or to the clan of one's father was prohibited and was believed to cause insanity. The clans were not ranked with respect to one another and served, at least historically, no apparent political function. Leadership was usually vested in an elder, who was considered by the group to be particularly qualified for the matter at hand.

Navaho ceremonials, or sings, as they are sometimes called, were also articulated along clan lines, but they tended to be much more particularistic than their Pueblo counterparts. Ceremonials such as the Squaw Dance were conceived primarily as a cure for an individual—the restoration of harmony between man and universe—whereas the ceremonials of the Pueblo were concerned more with the perpetuation and the well-being of society as a whole.

Traditionally the Navaho depended far more on family and clan ties for their cooperative activities than on friends and neighbors. As these two groups tended to overlap, this differentiation would be of only academic interest were it not for the fact that such new social aggregates as Little Bluff, where opportunities for wage work in nearby schools, hospitals, and administrative centers as well as for farming have forced a heterogeneous population of diverse social affiliation into sedentary life. The two hundred and fifty-odd inhabitants of Little Bluff— their number varies greatly throughout any one year— whose traditional social organization was congruent with a scattered settlement pattern and with frequent shifts of residence, now find themselves living in conditions which demand a single residence in comparatively close quarters with others to whom they cannot relate along traditional lines of kin and clan membership.

Although the response to this new life style has depended by and large on the individual Navaho, certain consistent patterns of adjustment are discernible. Little Bluff, recognized as a discrete geographical entity, is not so readily recognized as a discrete social entity. It is less a community than an aggregate of unrelated camps. Its inhabitants were attracted to the area by farming conditions —there is water—and the possibility of work in the nearby service community of School House.* The older

---

* A service community is essentially an artificial aggregate of ranch houses, hogans, trailers, and huts which have been built up around various government agencies and institutions, such as schools, hospitals, and land offices. There are usually a trading post, some restaurants, a greasy spoon, several garages, and often a Navaho chapter house.

people still relate themselves to the area where they were born (i.e., their mother's camp) or to the area where they or their relatives have sheep camps. The younger people identify more easily with School House, where they or their friends in fact attend or have attended school. Analyses of patterns of cooperation suggest that, although geographical proximity and friendship, as well as local commercial relations, are replacing considerations of family and kin, there is still a strong preference for the latter, especially in traditional activities such as ceremonials.

Even before coming to the reservation, I had been intrigued by the idea of writing a psychological profile of an "ordinary Navaho" who was moderately acculturated. A number of life histories of Navahos and other Indians have been collected, but, for the most part, these have been the lives of either very traditional or rather exceptional men. I hoped to present life-history material in the context in which it was given—and not in an edited form —and to combine this material with reports of the daily life of the informant. It seemed to me that, by combining the life history as conceived by the informant with a specific record of his behavior as conceived by the anthropologist and congruent with the anthropologist's own manner of perceiving and organizing reality, it would be possible to narrow the semantic gap which so often separates the members of one culture from those of another— even when the language they speak is the same.

Forster Bennett is a Navaho in his middle fifties. He grew up in a generation of children who, in his part of the reservation, were seldom educated in white man's schools and many of whom, like Forster himself, lost their parents in the influenza epidemic of 1918 and were raised by relatives. Of average intelligence and capacity—"white men think he's stupid and Navaho think he's smart"—he learned to read and write, but he has never developed a sophisticated understanding of the white man's ways. He has learned the behavior of the white man but has never really fathomed the subtlety of his motivation. (It should be pointed out that most white men who pride themselves on their Indian savvy have as little comprehension of the motivation of the Indian.) There is a statuesque quality to Forster's perception of the white man's world—a sort of blunted expectation—which gives his behavior vis-à-vis the white man a dulled tone. There is also a schoolboyish quality to his posture toward the white man which often camouflages the fact that he himself is a very willful man. Unlike most Navahos of his generation, he has had a very consistent work record even though he has made no attempt to get a better job. This willfulness, which is reflected in such small incidents as the replacing of fence posts, is perhaps most apparent in his strong sense of responsibility toward his children.

Forster's family situation is, by Navaho standards, unusual. He moved to School House before he was married and remained there. His wives all came from the general area, and he established himself as a sort of suburbanite in Little Bluff before most of the other wage workers moved there. Unlike most of his neighbors, he has taken pride in his house and is conscious of his social position as a comparatively wealthy, educated man. Superficially there is nothing remarkable about his several marriages and the number of children he has, but the fact that he has undertaken to care for and educate them without the help of a woman in the house is rare. Forster feels the need for a woman in his house, and this fact should not be forgotten when considering his relationship with Sally and other young women. Although he is often whimsical and arbi-

trary with his children, he is, in my opinion, a good father.

The importance of Forster's military experience also
cannot be underestimated. (He served during World War
II, along with three thousand six hundred other Navahos.) Not only is the experience of war always an intense
one in itself, but for the Navaho the war was also an initiation into the wider world, and it gave them one of their
few opportunities to live with the white man on equal
terms. Most Navahos are very proud of their service in the
military, where for once they could be true to their own
tradition and yet identify at the same time with the white
man. Forster was especially proud of his military career,
but it was significantly marred for him by his constant
contact with the dead and by the fact that his brother, of
whom he was very jealous, made a higher rank than he
did. Forster's jealousy of his brother receives only a passing mention in my journal but would probably have
played an important role at a deeper level of analysis.

Forster's intensive contact with the dead of Guadalcanal
was one of the most traumatic experiences in his life. Traditionally the Navaho have feared the ghosts of the dead
with whom they have been in contact, and their ceremonial system has several sings designed to eliminate these
spirits. For those Navahos who have come in contact, as in
warfare, with non-Navaho dead, the ceremonial known as
Enemy Way or Squaw Dance is traditionally employed.
After World War II many Navaho veterans had this sing,
but, as far as I was able to determine, Forster, who had
had much more contact with alien dead than most Navahos, never had Enemy Way performed for him. He admit-
ted to having a Blessing Way—a rather less complex ceremonial whose ostensible purpose is the invocation of
blessings and the averting of misfortune—at the begin-

ning and the end of his term of service. However, he never specifically denied having had Enemy Way, and this ambiguity must be considered not only with respect to his attitude toward me, a white man, but also as a symptom of his own ambivalence toward the traditional Navaho religion. Whether he did or did not have an Enemy Way sung over him is not important; the point is that he did not have sufficient confidence in the sing for it to be entirely effective. His contact with white man's Christianity had undermined his confidence in his own Navaho religion, but it was not strong enough to dispel his traditional fears or to provide him with a new way of coping with them. (Forster is like many other Navahos in this respect.) And so it is not without significance that, both before I came to Little Bluff and after I left it, Forster permitted others—the following September it was his close friend Harold Kennedy—to use his land for the performance of Enemy Way. It is possible for those who attend another's Enemy Way, particularly if they undergo the secret blackening ceremony, to obtain some of the benefits of the sing. He used a similar subterfuge during the summer I was with him—when he visited the Shooting Way and partook of the herbal waters and sacred corn mush.

The fact that Forster could not obtain relief for traditionally inspired anxieties from either the Navaho or the white man's religion was to color my relationship with him, and this underlines the extent to which an anthropologist enters and often alters the situation he is studying. It seems likely that Forster's first mention of his military service was his way of properly introducing himself to me—his way of establishing his identity and importance with respect to the white man's world. Since I too had once been in the army, we had something important in common from the start. As time went on, however, Forster's war stories began to change drastically in tone and character. He seemed to be seeking catharsis. By the end of my summer there, he was repeating his stories almost compulsively, and each time they were more emotionally charged. At one level I had become a sort of confessor for him. I imagine that at the time he received some relief from this relationship. It seems unlikely, though, that the relief was more than temporary, as our relationship was not structured along therapeutic lines.

If my relationship with Forster was at one level that of a confessor, it was at another level that of the white man, who was responsible in the first place for his condition. As an intruder into his life, I was naturally resented at first and later probably became a focus—at some level of his consciousness—for the resentment which he felt for all white men and which he vividly expressed the day he told me that he had known my (imaginary) friend Pete Phelps, who was hated by the Navaho and was now dead. This fantasy had developed in another context, and it is directly related to Forster's other significant problem: his waning sexuality. The war dilemma may be seen as typically Navaho, exemplifying, as it does, the contradictory effects of acculturation on the Navaho. But Forster's concern with his sexual prowess cannot be seen in such general terms because the Navaho tend to accept their sexual lives with a great deal of realism and far less anxiety than most white middle-class Americans. Here we are dealing with an idiosyncratic problem, the response to which may or may not be typically Navaho.

Forster had suffered a great deal because of his former wives. His third wife, whom he seemed to have loved much more than the others, had been killed in an automobile accident—I never had the courage to ask him who was driving. He divorced the others. He consistently denied the existence of his last wife—it was the mention of his wife that triggered his fantasy about my friend—and she obviously had wounded him deeply. Although Forster had very likely been running after teen-age girls for years —he had even married one—he probably became compulsive about them only after his last wife deserted him. It was a sort of desperate attempt to regain what had been taken away from him, and if one considers (and here I have little corroboratory evidence) possible Oedipal complications, what was forbidden him; it is significant that most of the girls he chased, including Sally, were not much older than his own daughters. Forster's drinking— which was probably exaggerated during my term in Little Bluff by the fact that Forster was on vacation and forced to stay at home both because of his children and his car problems—was, in my opinion, largely a response to his sexual problems. It is noteworthy that he usually got drunk when confronted with the possibility of intimate contact with a young woman. Here again, I seemed to become both a confessor for him and an object for his resentment—both as a rival man and as a white man who, as a "superior," was responsible for his sexual problems. To Forster, at any rate, I was much more than a passive observer on the scene. My presence may have pushed him to break with Sally, much as it had encouraged him to put in for a water line to Little Bluff.

The fact that, to a considerable extent, I was wittingly or unwittingly drawn into the life of Forster and his family as well as of the other Navahos of Little Bluff was primarily responsible for my choice of the journal form for this book. I found that a journal provided a temporal framework through which changes in my informants' behavior and in my own perception could be recorded. To have ignored such changes would have resulted in a very distorted picture of Little Bluff and its people and would have altered the experience of "field work" beyond recognition. To have written an account of Forster's life, for example, in the standard life-history form would have been like putting together a jigsaw puzzle in which none of the parts exactly fit. Much of the behavior that was most revealing of Forster's character had little bearing on his life as a whole. To have "molded" him into one theoretical perspective or another would have been impossible. I simply did not have the data. The relationship between the anthropologist and his informant is quite different by nature from that between the psychologist and his subject or the psychotherapist and his patient. The juggling of relations between the therapist and the patient usually occurs within a socially prescribed situation; the anthropologist's relationship to his informant is not so readily given. He is a naïve intruder into the informant's culture, and his status is often determined for him before he is aware of it. In fact, one of the most irritating features of field work is the discovery of the limitations placed upon you by the status the people you are studying have given you.

The Navaho of Little Bluff had had too much experience with white men to provide me straightforwardly with the sort of kin role anthropologists working in less sophisticated situations often have assigned to them.* It would be a mistake, however, to assume that I was not cast in some kin role at less conscious levels (transference). Both Forster and his son John related to me in kin terms in this sense. Forster's relationship to me, as I have said, was highly ambivalent—I was both father confessor and white man to him, and probably also in some ways a son. John

* There was, however, the superficial association with Forster's family—often my best introduction to other Navahos.

picked up on the latter role; much of his relationship with me can be seen in terms of sibling rivalry. To what extent I myself responded to this (counter-transference) is difficult to determine. The dreams I had on the reservation certainly suggest I did.

Field work is a very human experience and, as such, a very difficult one. Participant observation—a sort of catchall for the anthropologist's method or lack of method —is tautologically interpreted as the anthropologist's participation in the culture he is observing. The function of the anthropologist is sometimes quite naïvely said to be to approximate the life of the native! Were his task simply to learn the skills of the people he is studying—hunting, weaving, woodcarving, and the like—such a superficial interpretation of participant observation would be satisfactory, but the job the anthropologist sets himself is not at all so simple. Anthropological analysis involves understanding the subtleties of the subject's relationships— relationships in which he inevitably becomes entangled and from which he must constantly extricate himself if he is to achieve any objectivity.

The anthropologist's dilemma is reflected in a certain ambiguity in the phrase "participant observation" itself. The anthropologist is expected both to be and not to be a participant in the culture he is observing. As an observer who translates what he sees into terms meaningful to himself and other members of his own culture, he cannot participate *fully* in the culture under study, and as a participant in the latter he cannot observe the culture in a completely detached, objective way.

Some anthropologists have attempted to side-step the issue entirely by espousing a crude behaviorism tempered with an even cruder philosophy of operationalism, and others have surrendered to the allure of the instrument—the camera, tape recorder, hemoglobinometer, and, most recently, the bugging device and the closed-circuit television set. Although all of these instruments have been and can be put to legitimate use in anthropology and other human sciences, they too are limited by a definite perspective and interfere with the lives of the people under study. And in the case of the bugging device—and I am not being glib—they interfere with the conscience of the investigator.

An anthropologist is involved, intimately involved, with the people he is studying at all levels of his consciousness. This is a given and must be accepted as inevitable. Field work has to be seen in its existential dimensions. An anthropologist is a man in confrontation with other men—and he affects and is affected by them indelibly. But the American anthropologist is also from a society which places great stock in whatever is objective and scientific and which is beginning to disregard the potentials of human flexibility, such as man's ability to enter into a wide variety of situations without ever succumbing to any of them so completely as to lose *him*self. This is the rhythm of the critic who moves from a state of suspended disbelief to a critical perspective, of the phenomenologist who brackets off momentarily the cultural biases of perceptual life, of the psychotherapist who empathizes with his patient, or of the con man sliding into his next role.

As a participant observer, then, the anthropologist is no longer in his own culture, subject to familiar social rewards and restrictions, nor is he fully in the culture of the people he is studying. He inhabits, emotionally, a sort of no man's land in which, if he is honest with himself, he discovers himself to be particularly vulnerable. In an alien culture which he does not understand and which he cannot find *fully* satisfying, he is usually unable even to approximate a dialogue, and he often gives in to a deep loneliness and depression. Moreover, facets of the culture can arouse deeply buried fears and anxieties in him. Fantasies and defenses are developed and elaborated in a frighteningly personal fashion, and these must be taken into account and understood. Many anthropological monographs have been little more than reifications of the author's fantasies or justifications of the defenses he has built up.

As a scientific investigator, an anthropologist is also caught up in an ethical dilemma. On the one hand, he wants to observe the culture he is studying under the purest possible circumstances, and on the other hand, he feels certain strong urges to interfere in the lives of his informants, especially when he believes himself capable of helping them. Most anthropologists are not immoralists, and yet they sometimes find themselves in situations analogous to that of Ingmar Bergman's author in *Through a Glass Darkly,* who watches with fascination, though not without pangs of conscience, as his daughter goes mad.

Psychological and ethical problems of field work, such as these, are compounded by the need to establish and maintain an intensive working relationship with people whom the anthropologist may or may not find sympathetic. Not only can problems of rapport tax the field worker's patience, especially when the people he is working with are, like the Navaho, mistrustful and slow to reveal themselves and their ways to strangers, but they demand a degree of restraint which can impose severe strains on his usual way of managing his emotional life.*

* Since my experience with the Navaho, I have worked with a group of Moroccan Arabs belonging to a religious brotherhood

When in Little Bluff on a training grant,* I was particularly lucky in that I had the freedom to experiment with different anthropological styles and techniques. But the one rule I forced myself to keep was absolute honesty in recording observations. At first I tried to keep two sets of notes—one set in which I recorded what I observed and a second which I devoted to my own emotional responses and theoretical confabulations—but this sort of distinction was impossible to maintain. It seemed artificial, and I found that punctuation alone was usually enough to differentiate observations from responses. I did continue to keep a private journal, as I had for years, but the few entries turned out to be almost entirely about art and literature. They served, I suppose, to reinforce my own cultural life at times when I felt it to be crumbling. They reveal nothing about the Navaho, and I have not included them.

The journal, as it now stands, is an edited version of my field notes.† It attempts not only to portray the daily life of Forster and the other Navahos of Little Bluff but to present in as faithful a way as possible the experience of doing field work. Nothing that was not already suggested in the notes themselves has been added in the book. All quotations are as exact as possible. The Navaho are not a talkative people, and even when note-taking was impossible, such as at meals or in a car, I found that I could eas-

---

known as the Hamadsha. The Hamadsha would often reveal themselves so quickly, and I would find myself experiencing such a rapid succession of anxiety reactions to them, that I had to slow down the pace of my interviews in order to maintain my objectivity at all.

* The field work upon which this journal was based was sponsored by the Tri-Institutional Field Training Program of the National Science Foundation.

† All personal and place names have been changed, as well as all facts that would reveal the identity of my informants.

ily remember what had been said. My greatest problem in recording Navaho conversation had less to do with content than with rhythm. Our system of punctuating to indicate speech rhythms depends largely on the reader's familiarity with the spoken language. But although many of the Navahos with whom I worked spoke English, the rhythm of their English was very different from what one normally associates with the language. Not only does a Navaho pause so long between phrases that were a speaker of standard American English to speak in the same way he would be regarded as being highly embarrassed, but he also often makes long pauses between individual words. This difference was brought home to me again in a conversation with an American diplomat in Morocco who had spent his boyhood near the reservation. As he recounted his experiences with the Indians, his voice changed, much to the puzzlement of some of his listeners, and the fairly rapid, modulated speech of an urban American became the slow, drawn out monotone of a reservation Navaho.

When, a year after my stay on the reservation, I finally found time to look over my journal to see what, if anything, could be done with it, I was surprised to find a certain rhythm to my entries. They were not the random, disjointed observations I remembered them to be, but rather a series of episodes which seemed to me to betray the flat, slow quality of reservation life. To what extent this was the result of my own predilection to perceive in dramatic terms, and to what extent this was the result of an underlying dramatic quality to Navaho life when it is experienced by an outsider, I am unable to say. It is certainly true, as Jean-Paul Sartre remarks, that the stream of experience becomes episodic only in retrospect. It is also possible that I tended to impose an episodic tone on the experience as a compensation for a sort of emotional deprivation I felt at the time.

Americans seem to have a great deal of difficulty accepting simply and comfortably, and not merely tolerating, the sort of social and psychological differences that Forster and the other Navahos in Little Bluff represent. Much has been written about the American's desire to conform, but far less emphasis has been placed on his ability to accept difference without anxiety. The results of this anxiety vis-à-vis the Indian are varied. It may lead to a distortion of the difference, as in the romanticizing of the Indian; to an attempt to modify the difference, as in certain missionary activities; to a denial of the difference, as in the identification of the Negro cause with the Indian one; to an "objective and scientific study" of the difference, as in some anthropological and sociological studies of the Indian; or to the destruction of the difference itself. Then, too, the anxiety may be recast in mythic terms, as when one speaks of the collective guilt of the American people toward the Indian.

The Navaho problem, like other Indian problems, is complex and cannot be solved by formulas and simplifications. Efforts to incorporate it into an essentially urban poverty program or to understand it in terms of the Negro civil rights movements only falsify the Navaho plight. Pressure groups seeking to protest the war in Vietnam, to fight urban poverty, or to lobby for Negro rights have begun to include the American Indian in their causes, less, it seems, out of any true understanding of the Indian problem than for political and propagandistic purposes. The extremes to which such incorporation has been carried are well illustrated by the case of The Original Great Springout: A Megalopolitan Peacepipe

Pow-Wow of April 15, 1967. Two loads of Sioux from North Dakota—the nearest group of Indians who were willing to attend—were brought to New York to lead a parade in protest against the war in Vietnam and afterward to attend a "traditional Indian peace pow-wow" in Central Park. Some Indians, to be sure, have jumped on the bandwagon, but they have done so, one suspects, less out of any deep sympathy for the particular cause than out of a desire to protest their own predicament in whatever way at hand. It would seem that any realistic, effective, and humane approach to the Indian must involve not only an analysis of the Indian's social and cultural patterns and the opportunities offered him in the United States at large but a conscientious examination of our own motives and attitudes.

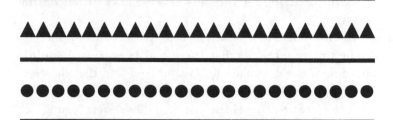

JUNE 27

I WAS NATURALLY APPREHENSIVE when we drove out to the Navaho reservation. I had never been on a reservation before, and, with the exception of an assistant Boy Scout troop leader I had known at the age of eleven, I had never spoken to an Indian.

Gene, an acquaintance who had lived on the reservation for years, had warned me earlier to expect changes in my perception in the desert. He was right. The desert, opening suddenly below us as the car climbed up and over a ridge, managed to obliterate every certainty of scale and space. It could have been a moonscape. It was the color of weathered rust, but it was splotched with green here and there until the reservation itself began. Then there was no more green—nothing to fix on, nothing to orient the eye. We were halfway through Little Bluff before I realized that we were there. I caught a fleeting glimpse of Forster Bennett's camp and the hogan in which

I would be living for the next seven weeks. It left no impression.

During the afternoon, a Hopi policeman stopped at Gene's place. He said that there had been an automobile accident a few days ago on Navaho land and that the Navaho police had refused to take the corpses away. Instead, they had called the Hopi police. "They were young fellows," he said, "and were afraid of the dead." Gene was not surprised. He said that the Navaho were traditionally afraid of the dead and avoided all contact with them. The older Navahos even refused to mention the names of their dead relatives.

After dinner we drove back to Little Bluff to Forster's gray cement-block house. Getting out of the car, I spotted two heads poking around the corner of the house and another at a kitchen window. Forster himself was sitting in an old, bent garden chair on a flagstone terrace by the door. He was a short, stocky man somewhere in his middle fifties. He made no attempt to rise. Gene and I both sat down on the terrace floor. There were no other chairs. Four or five minutes passed in silence.

"Two women stay here now," Forster said finally. "Their baby very sick and in hospital for one week. Measles, pneumonia, diarrhea. Maybe you come back tomorrow. Women leave tomorrow."

Before I had a chance to say anything, Gene suggested that I sleep out on the terrace. Forster did not seem very anxious for me to spend the night there.

"There are plenty of mosquitoes here at night," he said.

I wondered why there would be mosquitoes in the desert, but I said nothing.

A truck drove up. The driver mumbled a few words in Navaho and walked over to the hogan where the two women were staying and where I was to have stayed.

"That man is uncle of baby. He find out if women stay," Forster explained. "Where you come from?"

"New Jersey," I said.

"I was in Texas. They sent me there. First to Texas, then to Arizona, and then to Boston. It was cold there, so cold. . . . I was put outside for two hours, at night. Very cold. Then I got sick and they send me to hospital. I was there for three weeks. I was lucky. My company, it goes to England, France, and maybe Germany. . . ."

Forster went on talking about his life in the army during World War II. Perhaps it was a way of introducing himself. He listed each place in which he had been stationed. After maneuvers in the Aleutian Islands, he had been sent to Washington for rest and recuperation.

"I receive furlough there. Five days not enough to go to reservation. Not for me. I go to Seattle. There on street, walking along, I see Shoshone girl. She was just like Hopi, not like Navaho. Navaho different." (Gene said later that Forster meant physically different, but I thought he was referring to the distinction he made between Navahos and all other Indians.) "We walked around a lot and then into little street. I call my wife on reservation. She does not know where I am. She thinks maybe in San Francisco." He laughed. "She send me plenty of money. They didn't pay me for three months. I can't understand it."

The Shoshone girl was apparently quite taken with Forster. She visited him at the military base and claimed to be his wife so that he could get a pass. She took him home, fed him noodles, and introduced him to her family. When he was shipped out to Hawaii, she was very upset and cried.

"She cry very much when I leave. In Hawaii they give me my pay, three months' pay. I can't understand why so long."

Forster talked about the Shoshone girl with very little emotion. His voice was flat, with almost no variation. Occasionally he laughed. He sounded a little like an army man bulling and, at the same time, like an old man reminiscing.

The man had still not come back from the hogan. Gene asked why he was taking so long. Forster went to find out and came back a few minutes later.

"The women, they stay," he said.

"OK, we'll come back tomorrow."

Gene said afterward that Forster did not want me to spend the night outside his house because he wanted to do things right.

JUNE 28

I SPENT MOST OF THE DAY talking to officials of the Bureau of Indian Affairs. They all seemed dull, and I couldn't really make out their attitude toward the Navaho. They seemed to know their way around the Indians without really knowing them. They were concerned about them, but I couldn't tell how much of this was just professional.

I looked for Forster at the school, where he works as a maintenance man, but couldn't find him, and so early in the evening Gene drove me back to Little Bluff. Forster and his fifteen-year-old son, John, were putting new seat covers on Forster's Ford. Unlike most Navahos, who drive pickup trucks, Forster drives a sedan. I wondered whether this was for prestige. He did not greet me but simply stated that they couldn't get the front seat out. I joined in.

Gene watched. After several futile attempts to get the seat out—I was anxious to make a good impression on Forster and his son, who was watching suspiciously—I stepped aside to let John try again. This time he removed it easily.

"Did you bring your bedroll?" Forster asked. It was a sign that there was a place for me. I answered that I had and got it from Gene's truck.

"There's no water. Something wrong with well. I don't know what. Maybe tomorrow we go to see." (Earlier, I had learned at the BIA offices that only a few camps in Little Bluff have running water, which they obtain by direct lines from artesian wells on the bluff itself.)

"Do you have barrels?" Gene asked. "We'll use the truck."

Forster seemed grateful. We loaded the truck with several rusty old steel drums and drove to a nearby well. Most of the drums leaked. When Gene finally left, I noticed that Forster did not thank him. We continued working on the car. Forster asked me again where I came from and then told me he had been in Pennsylvania. He did not like it because it was too cold.

A car pulled up. Two young Navaho men got out. One was Forster's cousin Bill Thomas. I don't know who the other was. He didn't say a word during the hour they stayed. Bill was very talkative, though. He told me that he had the same job as Forster, who was going to retire soon. Forster grunted, expressionless.

"There's no water. Even Mr. Berger," he said, referring to Gene, "he come with big truck and we get water."

"You'll have to drink wine," Bill laughed. "The trouble with the Indians is that they drink too much. There is fifty per cent alcoholism. The people bring back a bottle of cheap wine for sixty cents and sell it for a couple of dollars. At next election they vote for permission to sell beer on the reservation. It's a good idea. That way the tribe will get the money."

Bill was showing off. He started talking about his job —Forster had evidently got it for him—and then about the farming problems in Little Bluff. In the old days, he said, the fields were green and splendidly farmed. There was plenty of corn and squash and peach and pear trees. Water was no problem. He assured me that Little Bluff had been a veritable Eden, and then, suddenly, he began complaining about a BIA training program to improve the farming that had failed "because the Indians didn't get the concept"—a phrase which he repeated several times. Any contradictions in his logic he chose to ignore. He invariably referred to the Navaho with a touch of scorn as "the Indians" or "they." Once he caught himself and apologized. "I'm talking about the hicks, the ones who don't live in the towns. Some Indians get one concept, but they couldn't get two. They learn to rotate crops but they still overgraze. Old Man Big Bead sometimes has two dozen horses grazing on his place." (The Big Bead outfit is the largest in the area. The old man, Gene had told me, is one of the most famous medicine men in the area.) "They're not stupid or illiterate. They just don't understand."

"There are too many white men coming around here lately," he said suddenly. "They come here for a week or so and then go back East and write their PHs and think they know everything." Bill was referring to me. He knew I was planning to stay two months. "Sometimes they stay two months and then go back," he added, making himself clear. And then—"It's getting late. I'm a working man. I got to get up early." He and his friend drove off.

Forster gave me the key to the hogan, where I made a

bed out of an old metal cot. There was no mattress. I went to sleep hungry. I hadn't eaten anything at Gene's, and Forster and his family had already eaten by the time I arrived. No mention was made of how much rent I was to pay or where I would eat.

JUNE 29

AT SIX FIFTEEN Forster knocked at the hogan door. He said he was going to School House in a half hour and would give me a ride. I washed and shaved quickly in water that tasted of kerosene. The smell of fried eggs filtered in from Forster's kitchen. I was dreadfully hungry. I walked over to the car and stood around. Forster came out, dressed in a heavily starched gray work uniform and a green cap.

"What you do about eating?" he asked.

"I thought I might be able to eat with you," I answered. "I'll buy the food."

"Some boys they stay here once, eat in hogan. They have big stove, Coleman stove." I didn't really know what Forster wanted me to do.

"I'd like to eat with you, if it's OK. I don't have a stove."

"The girls do the cooking."

"What kind of food do you want me to buy?"

"Anything you like. Maybe some potatoes," Forster said, a little embarrassed, "and oranges and coffee, the powdered kind. Anything you like. Maybe some chopped meat."

Forster, John, and Lana, his seventeen-year-old daughter, and I all piled in the car. John seemed much thinner than I remembered. He was dressed in a pair of tight black jeans, shredded at the cuff, a brown-and-orange-striped polo shirt, and black, pointed, ankle-high shoes. He smelled strongly of cheap after-shave lotion. I noticed that he had no beard. Lana was beautiful. She was dressed neatly in a white blouse and a gray skirt. Her sleek black hair was carefully done up in some sort of pouf. She was disturbing and was obviously aware of it.

I hitched a ride back and dropped the food off in my hogan. The kitchen was locked. I wondered how I would spend the day and decided to map Forster's land and inspect his buildings. His camp seems to be one of the largest in Little Bluff; he has fenced in more than an acre. There are three hogans, the one I occupy and two others used for storage, a lean-to garage which is filled with junk, a flimsy arbor off the back of the house, and the house itself. It consists of four rooms—three bedrooms and the kitchen—all with separate entrances. Five trees are planted in a row in front of the house to provide shade.

Big Bead's camp consists of a row of seven or eight houses in various states of disrepair and a few old trailers, all sheltered by large trees. Fifteen horses and a colt were grazing on an acre of the greenest land in Little Bluff. As I walked through the camp, I was eyed suspiciously by the various members of the Big Bead family, who were eating under the trees or in the trailers. Everything was dirty. Flies were buzzing around everywhere. The old man was seated at a table with two of his sons, and his daughter-in-law was sitting on an old bedframe with two baby girls, dressed in dirty gray undershirts and no diapers, who were playing with the springs. They were all eating greasy fried bread (the Navaho's unleavened, deep-fried bread) and drinking orange or grape pop. The old man was very picturesque. He had a long wizened face and dark intelligent eyes. He wore turquoise earrings—his earlobes were stretched by their weight like the ears of old southern Italian peasant women—and a long necklace of rough chunks of turquoise. Some were the largest I had ever seen. I suppose that's where he got his name.

My introduction seemed superfluous. The old man had heard my line before, according to his son Tom, who translated for him. A white man had come by a few weeks ago with some pictures and had asked the old man to tell him stories about them. Afterward, he offered to pay. The old man refused. It was clear that he resented the stranger *and* his offer. "There are too many secret agents around here," he said. Tom explained that his father was happy to be my friend but that he did not want to talk to me about his practice. Language was the big problem, he said. The sings (the Navaho ceremonials) had to be understood perfectly to be understood at all. Even he, Tom, was at a loss with most of the words in them.

"It's like going from kindergarten to university," his brother interrupted. "In university you learn many words you never knew before."

"Maybe you speak to my brother Freddy," Tom suggested. "Maybe he help you. He knows a lot about these things. But I don't think he will. How long you stay here?"

"Two months or so."

"Two months is not a very long time to understand his trade—medicine man," Tom continued. The old man nodded in agreement; I wondered how he understood. "To understand, you need a year. Writing things down in a book is no good. You must go out and do it."

"The sings are very complicated," the old man said. "You see those rocks." He pointed to the bluff. "Just as there are many different rocks, which are all important, in the cliff, so it is with my work. Every part counts. Every part is important."

I was overwhelmed. I hadn't said anything about learning a sing. I was just interested in talking to him. I decided to change the subject and ask about his family.

"My parents are dead," he said, "so you can't know them. I was just like a lizard. I left home when I was three and didn't know my parents." And then, "A lot of anthropologists, they come here and they say they want to be my friend, and then they go away and put down what I say in books and make a lot of money."

"I don't know about other anthropologists," I told him. "When I tell someone that I want to be friends, I mean it."

"What you going to do with what I tell you?" he asked. And before I could answer he said, "Anthropologists, they make a lot of money on what I say."

"If I published anything you told me . . ."

"I don't want to be paid," he announced proudly. He was arguing for argument's sake, and there was a twinkle in his eye. Sitting there at the table, with his sons around him and all his jewelry on, he made a perfect old potentate. I told him I wanted to be his friend, regardless of whether or not he wanted to talk to me about himself, and that I'd come back soon to visit if it was all right with him. He said it was.

As I approached Freddy Big Bead's place, I had the impression that he had been warned about my coming. I found him squatting in the corner of the kitchen of his half-finished clapboard house sewing moccasins. It seemed a cliché. We talked easily about his family and life in Little Bluff. His English was excellent.

"You don't own land. You just use it. Some people have

a small patch. They plant melons and corn. If the crop fails, they go hungry. They live the best they know how. No pensions. No work on account of education. Like me, never went to school. I learned to speak English in the army. I don't know how to write but I know my right." He laughed. "I don't mean my right in the way of the law. I mean my right hand. Too many rights! Right Face. Left Face."

He had been in the South Pacific from 1942 to the end of the war. There was something very smooth about him and he knew, I felt, exactly how to handle me. He did explain that the old man had once dictated a complete sing to an anthropologist, who had then published it without so much as sending back a copy. As I was leaving I asked him how he had known I was coming. He was not surprised by my question.

"The kids ran over and told me. I said, 'What do you expect? Where there's a medicine man, there's an anthropologist.' "

Dinner consisted of chopped meat, potatoes, and corn, all fried together, and plenty of sliced white sandwich bread. John drank Hawaiian punch, Forster and I coffee. The girls, who had prepared the meal, ate separately under the arbor. I've not yet had a chance to talk to Martha and Cora, Forster's youngest daughters. They seem very shy, almost afraid of me.

There was still no water. At dinner I asked Forster if he had found out whether anyone else was having trouble with water. He hadn't. We loaded the car with shovels, picks, and other tools—I was astonished by the number of tools he had stashed away—and drove around to the top of the bluff, where the well which feeds Forster's line is located. We stood around for a few minutes, not knowing what to do. From a nearby hogan, a woman watched us. John finally climbed up to the top of the tank and announced that it was empty. Forster shook his head and, after a few minutes, slowly walked over to the woman, who told him that a man named Grant usually inspected the wells.

We headed toward Grant's place but stopped on the way to say hello to Dermot Lewis, a friend of Forster's who works for the BIA. Later I found out that he was a member of Forster's clan. Forster seemed reluctant to see Grant, and as we drove up to his cement-block house, he pointed to a "Don Alexander" sticker on Grant's car. A torn "Robert Arthur" sticker is pasted on the rear bumper of Forster's Ford. Don Alexander is the Old Guard candidate for Navaho tribal chairman, Forster told me later, and Robert Arthur the Young Guard candidate. Arthur is for "education and progress." I did not really think that Forster's reluctance to see Grant had anything to do with this political difference.

A neighbor, who was building a flagstone patio, told Forster that Grant was in and to go around to the back door. Standing carefully to the side of the screen door, Forster knocked, and only when there was no answer did he look in through the door. No one was there. We walked to the front of the house. Grant and his wife asked us in. They were sitting on shabby brown couches in a large living room where a pug was playing with a little blue plastic football. They seemed better off than Forster.

Forster introduced me to Mr. and Mrs. Grant, who talked to us in English. Grant, an elderly man dressed in blue denim overalls and a blue work shirt, explained that there was nothing he could do about the well itself. His job was to maintain the water lines, not the wells.

"The wells go clear down to China," he said. "The people in Little Bluff should have water from the main line, but it's their own damn fault. They voted against it. The same thing happened around here. It took us thirty years to get water. The people didn't understand. When they finally got water, they thought they wouldn't have to pay. Well, they got three months' water free. That was all. Then they had to pay. Many of them moved away. I don't understand it. They pay two dollars for a pint of wine and then another two, and then they are drunk and buy a third. So they spend six dollars but they won't spend a couple of dollars for water."

Forster and Mrs. Grant listened attentively. Occasionally she would nod her head in agreement. I could not make up my mind whether Grant himself resented paying for the water. He told Forster how to go about getting tribal action for a main line to Little Bluff. He outlined each step carefully. It was necessary to have a petition signed by the local chapter president, vice-president, and secretary and then hand it in to the Sanitation Department.

"Then they send them to Window Rock and then to Washington. Maybe in a year, maybe in six months, maybe never, you get water," Grant said resignedly.

Forster suggested that maybe Dermot could help. Grant shrugged his shoulders.

The talk about water went on for another fifteen minutes. Grant repeated himself a good deal, putting more and more emphasis on the need to have the petition signed and submitted, and finally got up and brought back the papers for the petition. Forster more or less agreed to have them signed.

"Tomorrow I take a look at the well," Grant said. "Maybe there's a vapor lock."

We left. John had remained in the car all this time. We

stopped at the houses of both the chapter vice-president and the secretary to have the petition signed. On the way back home, Forster talked excitedly about progress—the future was with the Young Guard—and education.

"You should be like him," he said to John, pointing at me. "He have plenty education. University and all. What name of university?"

"Columbia," I said.

"Yes, that's right. Columbia University," he said, dropping the second *i* in university.

I wondered how John felt about this comparison.

When we arrived at the house, Forster told me about his neighbors—their names and clans—and later he and his family came into my hogan to help me fix it up. We improvised a mattress out of old clothes.

JUNE 30

FORSTER AND I DROVE TO Round Point, an administrative center about thirty miles from Little Bluff, very early in the morning to have several leaking water drums welded. On the way the windshield wipers broke. (It was drizzling.) We stopped at Joe's garage to have them fixed.

"I have some water tanks," Forster said to Joe, a white man, after the wipers had been repaired; "they need welding. I try to get them fixed someplace else. If not, maybe I come back."

"Yes, you can come back," Joe said.

"You come and look at them," Forster suggested.

"I thought you were going to take them someplace else," Joe answered dryly.

"I changed my mind. It's easier this way."

The laundromat was crowded. Forster decided to take the wash into Carteret, where there would be no waiting. It is well over a hundred miles from Little Bluff.

At 9:30 a.m. Mr. Grant stopped by to find out if the water was working. It was. He had gone to repair the well immediately after we had spoken to him last night.

I spent most of the day visiting families in the neighborhood and had a difficult time. The people in Little Bluff seem very wary of white men. Like Old Man Big Bead, they manage to make me feel as though I've giving them a line which they have all heard before. It undermines my confidence. I plunge right into an interview without giving them time to get used to me and then always have the feeling that I am talking too fast and too much. It's also hard to avoid looking into the eyes of the person I'm interviewing. Language is going to be a problem. Fewer Navahos speak English than I expected. The important thing, I guess, is just to take it easy and let word of my presence get around. Living with Forster seems to be the best introduction of all.

Roger Cole: He lives in a camp of two clapboard cabins and a hogan. Roger, a tall Indian in his early fifties with heavy eyelids, was sitting on a wooden box in the corner of one of the clapboard houses. The place was filthy. A dirty baby was playing on some pink and green blankets heaped up in the center of a metal bedframe. This was the

only piece of furniture. Roger's wife was seated on the floor
before a loom, on which she was weaving a black-and-
white rug. She was very slovenly. Roger seemed to be in a
stupor (or suffering from a severe hangover), from which
he would emerge occasionally to eye me mistrustfully.
Roger's wife spoke enough English to tell me that neither
she nor her husband understood what I was saying and
she pointed to the second clapboard house, indicating that
there was someone there who would understand.

I walked over slowly and knocked, standing to the side
of the open door. In a few minutes, a young woman carrying a baby came to the door. She had obviously been
pretty as a girl, but she had aged rapidly and seemed very
shy. Her name was Sheila. She told me that she was
twenty-seven and had three children, and then—after a
good deal of hesitation on her part and prodding on mine
—that she had been married twice and was separated
from her second husband. She seemed very embarrassed
by this. I asked her about Roger Cole. She said he was her
"uncle" and blushed. I immediately suspected that Sheila
was Roger's second wife, that is, until I learned that
they were of the same clan. This would preclude such an
arrangement, since marriage between clan brothers and
sisters is considered incestuous. This relationship seemed
unlikely, and yet there was something strange about the
whole setup. She lived alone with her three children in a
house in a clan brother's camp about fifty miles from her
mother's place.

Colin Curtis: Colin's camp, which is clean and neat, consists of a wooden two-room house, an arbor, and a second
house which he is in the process of building. He has no
running water but hopes that a line will soon be put in;
he does have electricity. He is a gentle man of medium

height, who greeted me warmly, led me into the arbor, and offered me a seat at a large table. His five daughters, the oldest of whom is nine, watched us inquisitively. His wife was away at work at a restaurant on the main highway. He does the baby-sitting during the day, but when he is at work—he works shifts at a garage—he has a girl come to help him. His wife can only come home on her day off. Colin seemed very interested in what I was doing and was anxious to help. I had considerable trouble understanding him because he speaks English with an unnerving staccato.

Willy Murphy: Willy lives in a wooden house just behind Tall Singer's hogan. I had planned to visit Tall Singer, an old medicine man, whom Forster had mentioned, but before I had a chance to, Willy came out of his house, asked me in very fluent English who I was, and then invited me into his bleached-wood cabin, which had a sink. Even Forster's house, which is one of the best in Little Bluff, does not have a sink—it has just a faucet. Willy is a thin man of sixty-seven with nervous eyes which seem never to settle on any single object. He seated himself on his bed, which was made with hospital corners, and pointed out a chair for me. He told me that he was willing to help me but that he didn't know too much about Little Bluff.

"I moved here about four or five years ago," he said with a drawl, "to help my 'brother' [Tall Singer] who's getting kinda old. He's seventy-eight years old. I'm sixty-seven myself. My brother couldn't take care of the fields, so I moved down here."

"Is Tall Singer your real brother?"

"No. We just call each other 'brother.' We're both *Tsinijini.*"

"What does that mean?"

"*Tsinijini* is what you white folks call a clan. Sometimes they just say *'cisini.'* "

I asked him if *Tsinijini* has any meaning.

"The way the old folks told it, there was a ridge of trees and green stuff, plenty of trees and bushes. Well, the people are named after it. It's also known as the Bear Clan. The bear lives right on the ridge where there are trees, so it's named the Bear Clan."

"How did you get the name Murphy?"

"That wasn't my father's real name. Since the white folks at school couldn't say my name, they just called me Murphy."

I asked Willy about his family.

"Tall Woman was my mother. Her husband was Big Hat. In those days my father and my mother had another daughter outside of Big Hat. So my father wanted that girl to be his wife. They came to an agreement that it was all right. [Willy meant that his father had married his stepdaughter—an arrangement which was not infrequent in traditional Navaho society.] My father was a policeman when everything was kinda hot, on the warpath. He was a policeman after Fort Sumner."

"Was your father at Fort Sumner?" I asked.

"No, he didn't go to Fort Sumner. Of course, I never did ask him." Willy paused for a few minutes. "I was kinda green then. I didn't ask him. Ethel was the daughter. She had one daughter by Big Hat. . . . My father sent us to school. He was urged by different ones. He had plans when we get out of school and try and do something for ourselves. Later he died. A horse killed him. In that time I was at school in Albuquerque. It was a non-reservation school."

Willy's mother remarried after the death of her husband but had no more children. His stepfather raised him and encouraged him to continue school. Later he married.

"I had two girls, and they died at birth. I got a boy. He has a cornfield around Nugget. His name is Howard Alan Murphy," Willy said with a flourish. "He was going to school the last time I heard of it. I don't know where, but he was going to school. My wife lives around Nugget. We're divorced."

"Is she married again?"

"She's married again. I don't know who. We're not supposed to know such things."

I learned that Willy is a Presbyterian and goes to church "once in a great while." He grows corn, melon, and squash. Even though they are irrigated, "there's not much luck this year." The summer has been very dry. This morning's drizzle was the first in weeks and had not even softened the caked earth. All of the farmers are complaining about the drought.

As I was leaving, Willy mentioned that he was "kinda short on smokes." I promised to bring him some on my next visit. I find his commercial approach a relief.

On my way back from Willy's, I passed Howard Lightfoot's house. Howard is the school accountant. His house is the largest in Little Bluff: a ranch house equipped with air conditioning and illuminated at night by several powerful spotlights. Howard was watching several men load a truck. After I had introduced myself, he offered to show me around. I asked him about the water problem in Little Bluff.

"I've wanted the people of Little Bluff to have water from the main line," he said. "I have made many reports on the situation. There is no organization here. Little Bluff forms a community, but there are no leaders. The local chapter is in School House. Nothing has been accomplished. No one takes the initiative. I've been pushing for water but no one in the community has pressed for it."

I thought of Forster. He had taken the initiative but had not consulted anyone else. I wondered how much my presence had influenced his decision to submit the petition, if in fact he would submit it. It still needed the chapter president's signature.

When I returned, Forster was sitting in front of the house. He and the girls had just returned from Carteret. He asked me where I had been, and when I mentioned Howard Lightfoot, he said, "I don't like people like him moving down here. He doesn't come from around here." Neither do you, I thought to myself. "He's for Alexander," he added. "I seen sticker on car."

We continued chatting. Forster told me that President Johnson had spoken today. "He speak about 1940, 1942, and 1945 but not about today," he said disapprovingly. "Our people are getting killed." I had learned earlier that a few local Navahos had been killed in Vietnam. "They say there are some secret agents around Red Mountain, but I think they students," he continued. I agreed with him. There were in fact some anthropology students at Red Mountain.

Harold Kennedy, who is married to Forster's half sister Lucille and according to Forster is a medicine man, stopped by at suppertime. Harold had also been to Carteret and had brought back a few pints of wine. Both men began to drink, Forster making some effort to hide his glass from me. Throughout supper Harold and Forster talked in Navaho. Harold knows no English, and Forster would translate for me occasionally. Harold wanted me to know that when he was a boy his father made him cut a hole in the ice and stay under for a very long time. Then he had to run for miles and miles. This made him a strong man.

"Do you know where the white people come from?" Harold asked.

I told him I didn't.

"He says he knows where the Navaho come from," Forster said. "Maybe he tell you after Pow-Wow. You go see him then."

The Pow-Wow is a Pan-Indian celebration sponsored every Fourth of July by the businessmen of Flagstaff. It usually ends in a big drunk. Although Flagstaff is more than two hundred miles away, Forster and most of the other Navahos I have talked to are planning to go.

The two men continued talking: meat is very expensive in Flagstaff; Forster intends to go to High Point to slaughter a sheep and take the meat to the Pow-Wow—his sister lives around High Point and herds some sheep for him.

"I want to talk to you," Harold said as we finished our coffee, "but white men forget the people who teach them. I work with white men, many white doctors. I cure councilmen. I cure people in big area, fifteen, maybe twenty-five thousand acres. I remember everything since I was eight," he added in a drunken boast.

We left the kitchen. There was a rainbow in the sky. Harold asked me if I knew what it meant and then told me that when the Navaho pray under it "it give them strength and force. They can win at horse races and beat the Hopi."

While Harold, Forster, and the girls all went for a ride, John and a boy friend listened to some pop tunes in John's room. Occasionally they would beat out the rhythm with some old drumsticks against the bunk bed. Later two teen-age girls came over to see Forster's daugh-

ters, and when they found they were out they joined the
boys in John's room.

JULY 1

I STOPPED AT ROGER COLE's again this morn-
ing. His thirteen-year-old daughter gave me his genealogy.
She referred to Sheila as "my female cross-cousin" but
could not establish exactly how she was related. Roger was
again squatting in the corner.

I bought some cigarettes at a trading post for Willy Murphy. A few Navaho men were loafing in front of the store
on a long wooden bench and a few others were standing
around inside. Occasionally one would walk up to a clerk
and ask for something—a pair of Levis, some rope, or a
lantern. One or two women, dressed in traditional long
fluted calico dresses, wandered through the self-service
food section of the store, picking out a can of Vienna sausages or a bag of sugar. By far the greatest activity was cen-
tered on the soda machine, where a clerk was occupied
full-time opening bottles of cheap pop and giving change.
I drank a bottle of lemon-lime as I examined the pawn
shelf of turquoise beads and silver bracelets. I could see a
pile of blankets in the back room which were probably
also pawned. Gene had told me that many of the old trad-
ers had gone bankrupt rather than sell the pawned goods
of their Navaho friends.
I introduced myself to the trader, a white man, who
drives around in a new Buick convertible and lives with
his wife in a run-down house behind the store. One of his
sons is married to a Navaho girl, who runs around the

store in very tight faded-black shorts with a sour but efficient expression on her face. I don't think she does much work. The trader and his son were not very friendly. I suppose they regarded me as still another Easterner, who comes and goes without ever understanding the Indian but convinced he does.

Willy was loafing on his bed, like an army sergeant, reading a coverless pulp magazine when I arrived. We talked about farming and then about Tall Singer. Even though he lives a few yards away from him and is his friend and relative, Willy was "unable" to tell me where Tall Singer's wife was and claimed not to know very much about "this ceremonial business." He can't say whether Tall Singer's medicine works. He and Tall Singer are going to the Pow-Wow together.

Willy had been a radio operator in the artillery during World War II. He talked in Navaho from the front lines to someone at the command post. Willy enumerated, much as Forster had done, all the places he had been sent to: Australia, New Guinea, Bayak, Orlando, and the Philippines.

"There was nothing to think," Willy answered when I asked what he thought of the army. "I was drafted. I couldn't say. . . . Like loadin' sheep. . . . Didn't know where we was going. . . . Had to do whatever we was told. . . ." Willy was almost free-associating. There were long pauses between these phrases, which were said in no less than five minutes.

"I was the first to be drafted," he continued, coming out of his last long soporific pause. "I was in the army before, right around 1926 to 1938. Then I left, but they drafted me as soon as the war started. They had my records at Fort Riley, Kansas. I was stationed at Fort Sill,

Oklahoma. I was in the band. Played three instruments: the cornet, the bass, and the alto. I was just about the only Navaho."

I wanted to know why he had enlisted in the army.

"I just wanted to go into the army," he said slowly, after a long pause.

When he was discharged in 1938, he returned to his mother's camp and married. I asked him about the people in Little Bluff.

"I don't have too many relatives here. I don't know too many families. There are quite a lot here. They're always moving back and forth. Some have sheep up in the mountains. There are no sheep down here. They just live here for a while. Quite a lot work in town."

Willy goes to town from time to time to visit friends. He tries to visit his "sisters'" camp every month. Although he doesn't have any sheep, his "sisters" do.

We heard a blasting noise. A jet had crashed the sound barrier.

"They're dropping a bomb. Just testing," he remarked.

I asked him what he thought about Vietnam.

"The United States has a right to join in and fight for democracy, their rights, knowin' how to live the right way. A lot of them are—what do you call it, that group, that organization—communists. The United States hates to see people get killed and suffer. They try to stop this war if they can."

Willy was tired. His mind was wandering. I asked him about Don Alexander and Robert Arthur.

"Pretty soon, you know, there will be communists around here. That's what I think," he announced. "Different ways of living, different rights, well, like law and order. An election is like a race horse. If Alexander wins, he will have to be our chairman." He yawned.

Willy excused himself. He had promised to help a friend build a sweat bath. This is a low mud hogan, I learned from Willy, which is heated by rocks laid over an open fire. The traditional Navahos sing special songs as they sweat themselves clean.

In the afternoon I visited the Big Bead camp. Freddy had worked all night and was asleep. The rest of the men were away. I asked two teen-age girls to tell me about their families. They were shy but cooperative; they did not seem to know very much about traditional clan and family structure. They had both been reading *Romance Comics*—Forster's daughters do also—and were dressed like typical lower-class American teen-agers. The difference between the dress of the Navaho teen-age girl and the adult woman is striking. The girls wear tight Levi shorts or short skirts—the mini skirt had not yet gained popularity anywhere in the Southwest—and cotton blouses. The women still wear the more traditional costume. It would be difficult to distinguish Lana by her clothes from any attractive Puerto Rican in New York. Of course she differs in most other ways. John teases her by calling her Miss America.

I suspect there is some sort of tension between Forster and Willy. When I told him that I had seen Willy again, he seemed bothered and told me that Willy drank too much.

Forster gave me his genealogy today. Even though I had known that the old Navahos refuse to name their dead relatives, I was quite surprised when he refused to tell me the names of his parents. "They have been dead for a long time," he said, "I don't remember." He has two brothers and three sisters. His oldest brother graduated from high school (Forster finished the first two years only) and is now a lay Presbyterian missionary. He has never married, and Forster has not seen him for several years. I don't think they get along.

Forster told me that he had been married three times. (This contradicts Gene, who assures me that he has been married four times.) He divorced his first and second wives, and his third, Laura, to whom he seems to have been very attached, died in an automobile accident in 1954. He had no children by his first wife; by his second he had two sons, Douglas and Forster Junior, and a daughter, Ellen. Both Douglas and Ellen are married and have children. Forster does not remember the names of his grandchildren. Junior is in the army in Germany.

Laura and Forster had five daughters and one son. With the exception of Kitty, the eldest, who is married and living with her husband, and Rita, who is working in Grand Canyon at a restaurant, all the children are spending the summer at their father's. Lana and John have jobs in town. During the winter only Martha, Forster's youngest daughter—she is twelve—and John live at home. The others are away at school: Rita, nineteen, and Cora, fifteen or sixteen, at boarding school in Utah, and Lana in Albuquerque, where she lives with a foster family. She seems to be the most "American" of the children.

Forster seems to miss an older woman in the house. He has to take full responsibility for his children. He must make sure that they get to work and back in the summer and to school and back in the winter. The laundry and the cooking have to be done, and the house must be kept clean. Cora and Martha do most of the household chores. John helps with the heavy work and the car, which seems in constant need of attention. It is a focal point in the family life. Forster's children are very obedient and seem shyer than the other Navaho children I've seen. Forster speaks to them in the imperative, and they never talk back. They accept what he has to say without expression, dully. With the possible exception of Lana, they show very little curiosity and do not impress me as being very imaginative. Cora seems the least intelligent and the most withdrawn. Martha has a lively spark in her eyes but is still very timid. They usually speak Navaho with a word or two of English interjected here and there. Forster does not praise them to their face but seems proud of John and told me that he works hard. "Yesterday he put seat covers on and today he fix trunk of car." He appears concerned about the "kids' " shyness.

As we were waiting for supper Forster called my attention to the traffic on the highway. "They are going to Pow-Wow," he said. My own impression was that there were in fact a few more cars than usual but that the majority were going in the direction opposite to Flagstaff.

After dinner Cora and two girl friends—there are always several more girls around than I can keep track of— returned with a Presbyterian minister from the town in Utah where she goes to boarding school. He is spending the summer on the reservation to learn Navaho. He walked over to Forster in a very deliberate manner, extended his hand, and saying hello in Navaho in a loud voice, gave Forster a hearty handshake. The Navaho just touch hands lightly when they greet each other. He then shook hands with me in a similar fashion and sat down. He told us that he really liked the *Diné* (literally, the people, the term the Navaho use to refer to themselves) and was finding out how intelligent they were.

"You cain't be stupid if you can speak a language like Navaho," he said. "It is so much more precise than English."

He gave a few examples. Forster listened patiently, occasionally smiling at his accent. The minister then asked me something in Navaho and seemed surprised, almost hurt, when I told him I couldn't understand, but he quickly covered himself by praising my English and asking me where I had learned it. When I told him New Jersey, he seemed even more surprised and asked me what I was doing there. Forster listened, amused. Only when I told him that I was born there did he realize that I was not Navaho. I wondered how many blue-eyed Navahos he had seen. He did not appear to be terribly embarrassed but rattled on about how wonderful the Navaho were and how awful the Mormons were.

"They consider the Indians to be inferior," he said. "I know. I come from a town which is ninety-seven per cent Mormon. They don't care about the Indians. Most of my people are Indians from the school."

After he had learned what I was doing on the reservation, he suggested that I write a history of the Navaho for high-school students. "The *Diné* should be proud of their tradition, not ashamed of it. Most of the young people don't know about their heritage. They are even forgetting their language." He turned for confirmation to Forster, who nodded blankly. He then lectured us on the number of Indians who had died and were dying for the United States and on the role of the Navaho in World War II.

"That man, he sure talk a lot," Forster said after he left. "We go see chapter president now. He sign papers." It was quite late. Forster had been patiently waiting all this time for the minister to leave.

On the way to the president's house, Forster harangued Martha and Cora, who had come along, on the advantages of education. They should not be so bashful with me but should learn from me because I "was educated man all the way from Columbi Un'versty." He became so engrossed in his subject that we almost drove off the road. The girls giggled in the back of the car, and Forster himself laughed.

The chapter president is a schoolteacher and lives in one of the neat little cottages provided for school personnel. All of them have television aerials. Forster introduced me to him and he signed the petition without asking any questions.

Forster seems to be both showing off and showing me off. This burst of political activity is, I am sure, for my benefit. He wants me to realize his importance and conscientiousness. He is acting in an "ideal way." The question is which "ideal way"—Navaho or white-as-perceived-by-Navaho. It is probably the latter.

JULY 2

LAST NIGHT FORSTER ASKED me if I wanted to go with him to his sister's camp at High Point to bring back a sheep for the Pow-Wow. I told him I did. We were to leave at eleven "so we would get there by noon," when his sister would be expecting him.

This morning at six thirty sharp, Forster, John, and I left for High Point. It was a relief to leave Little Bluff, where I feel hemmed in, more, I suppose, by the lack of a car than by geography. As we drove out onto the plain, my eyes were opened once again by the vast expanse. It was like taking a deep breath. I felt relaxed for the first time since I arrived.

On the way the conversation turned to the Pow-Wow. Forster told me that he didn't like Pow-Wows. "There are so many people. They all drink too much. Get sick. Lots of fights. Everything dirty." He wouldn't go today if it weren't for the kids. Every time a car passed, regardless of its direction, Forster would announce that it was headed for the Pow-Wow. When John started saying the same thing, I began to wonder whether this was a figure of speech—or whether the Pow-Wow so dominated their attention that they were in fact seeing things differently.

We turned off the highway onto a dirt road, which was in fact little more than a track. Forster seemed to know his way over these, to my mind, indistinguishable tracks, but finally even he made a mistake. We came to a stranger's hogan and sat in the parked car directly in front of it for no less than five minutes—the people in the hogan ignored us and went about their business—until Forster asked them where his sister's place was. It was just beyond a dip in the road. As we approached the camp, which nestled in the hollow of two converging hills and consisted of two hogans and an arbor, Forster remarked that there were visitors. A pickup truck with Utah plates was parked in front of one of the hogans. This seemed both to surprise and upset him. He claimed that he did not know who the visitors were, but it was clear from his expression that he did. A man was chopping wood at the side of one of the hogans and a woman, Forster's half sister, was working under the arbor, which served as a porch for the second hogan. She looked up for a moment and then continued her work. Forster greeted her with a single word. Although they seemed happy to see each other, there was no exaggerated show of feeling. She was a thin, handsome woman whose voice had a charming lilt to it, which I'd also noticed in other Navaho women's voices. When she addressed me in English, I was surprised—misled, I suppose, by her traditional costume. She just looked at John but did not say anything to him. After she had told Forster in Navaho that the sheep were just over the ridge, she got in the car with us and drove to the flock, which was tended by a boy of about twelve and a dog. The five of us rounded up the sheep—there were about seventy-five— and looked for one which was marked with a red band. Forster looked it over and said it was not very fat, but he took it anyway. John and I tied its legs together and dumped it into the trunk of the car, along with a few cedar branches for firewood, and we drove off, leaving Forster's half sister about a mile from her camp. Not a word had been said to the herder or to John.

We returned at nine thirty. Forster was proud of the time we had made. We removed the sheep from the trunk as the girls gathered around to watch. Everyone was excited. Forster looked over in the direction of Harold Kennedy's camp, barely visible in the distance, and then told me I "could go and read or study." I was touched by his tact, but told him that I would prefer to help. He cut the animal's throat and collected the thick, warm blood in a white enamel pan. When I asked him whether the Navaho use the blood for anything, he assured me they didn't. This is strange, because the Navaho make blood sausages. I wondered if he felt ashamed. The girls left the blood on the table under the arbor and later in the day, when we were gone, Forster's two dogs, Blackie and the one that looks like a coyote and has no name, ate it up. Just as Forster was about to begin the actual butchering, an old man, a medicine man, Forster said, whose name he had forgotten but who was a member of his clan, appeared and made quick work of the animal with his pocketknife. Forster seemed relieved by his arrival, but told me that he hadn't expected him. The butcher, I learned later, lives with Harold Kennedy, with whom Forster had discussed his plan of slaughtering a sheep before the Pow-Wow began. I do not know whether or not it was actually arranged for this man to come. The whole butchering operation took about fifteen minutes. Forster assured me that a fast worker could do it in five. I was at any event very impressed by the butcher's skill—not a single slip of the knife, not a moment's hesitation.

While the butchering was taking place, the girls, who had been told to clean the kitchen, mopped the floor, emptied the slop pail, and moved the kitchen table out onto the terrace. Three chairs, and a stump and garbage can to serve as chairs, were placed around it. A fire was built in the stone fireplace under the arbor and the sheep's head, a great delicacy, Forster assured me, was thrown into the flames. Although Forster has both electricity and water, the only kitchen appliances he has are a large refrigerator and a toaster. The girls do the cooking on the fireplace. The liver, the intestines, and a sort of sausage, a special delicacy called *achii*, which is made by twisting the intestines around long strips of fat to make them look like macaroni twirls, were all fried in lard. At eleven we all sat down at the table and feasted. The *achii* wasn't bad at all. It was a big occasion. Even the girls ate with us.

After lunch, Forster pointed to the firewood and explained that they were piñon logs and made the best fires. He asked me if I wanted to go with him to get some more. I agreed. About an hour later Martha, Cora, John, and I got in the car and drove well over fifty miles into a national forest, where we finally stopped on a high plateau. I wondered what would happen if a ranger stopped us. Forster and I chopped wood while the kids, as Forster calls his children, collected it and loaded it into the trunk of the car. I was astonished by Forster's endurance. We were at an altitude of over six thousand feet and each stroke of the ax was for me almost my last—John eventually took my place as I shamefacedly joined the girls in loading the car—but Forster pushed on without a pause. When the trunk was full—how much handier a pickup truck would have been—we started back. The kids all fell asleep. I felt very parched and told Forster that I would treat everyone to soda at the first possible place. We proceeded in silence until we came to a deep gorge. Here, Forster told me, a few years ago a family had stopped to look at the view, and their car with their two children in it—the parents had stepped out—rolled over.

"Brakes no good," he explained. "Man and woman begin to fight. She want to jump over side after kids. When they take her to hospital, she can't hear. It must be terrible for parents to see their kids die like that."

He asked me a few minutes later what New York was like. He wanted to know whether there were big canyons and sheep and livestock. He was most interested in the weather, especially the rain. I told him about Central Park. He seemed puzzled that no one grazed sheep there until I told him it was illegal. We passed several Navaho police panel trucks. They were all going to the Pow-Wow, Forster said, "to enforce order." They herd up all the drunks in a big corral and hose them down with cold water. As we approached a trading post, I reminded Forster that I was treating everybody to soda. I'm sure he would have driven by had I said nothing. He parked the car in front of the motel, some distance from the trading post, and I walked over to the store alone. When I returned with the pop, he pointed to a soda machine in the motel and said, "I thought you go there. It cheaper."

Dinner was again a big occasion. Joan and Nancy Shepard, two friends of the girls, who live nearby and whom Forster is going to take to the Pow-Wow, ate with us. Forster complained about Navaho drinking and then with a curious admixture of prescience and fatalism said, "Tomorrow at this time I be drunk." Everyone laughed.

JULY 3

EVERYONE WAS EXCITED at breakfast. Joan and Nancy had spent the night. All the girls sleep in the bedroom behind the kitchen on a double bed and a couch. Last night there were five of them. Forster said that maybe he would see Sally at the Pow-Wow. He had heard she was coming. He has mentioned Sally once or twice. She seems to be his girl friend, though I don't think everything is well between them. She spent quite a bit of time with him this last spring but then left the reservation to work at a factory. Once, when he was complaining about his daughters' bashfulness, Forster told me that Sally wasn't "like that at all. When she come here to stay, she answer all your questions. She show you how to make fried bread. Not like these girls."

Breakfast was finished in record time. The trunk of the car was loaded with pieces of raw mutton wrapped in newspaper, bags of potatoes and oranges, a gallon jug of water, and several bedrolls. At the last minute Forster threw in his pillow. They were going to camp around the car. He gave me the keys to the house and apologized for not taking me.

"No room," he said. "I have to take kids. I tell them long time ago."

I assured him it was all right. Everyone squeezed excitedly into the car. As they drove off, I felt let down. I suppose I had been carried away by their excitement.

I'm finding the small differences in life style much more unsettling than the big ones such as religion and politics. Take, for example, the lack of praise. Forster tells John to do something, and John does it without a word. Forster neither thanks him nor praises him. It is taken for granted that he is grateful, just as it is taken for granted that the boy will do his best.

The Navaho just don't talk much. They seldom use such expressions as "thank you," "please," or "hello." They assume much of what we say. When I thank a Navaho for something, I have the feeling that I am uttering superfluities. To say hello is absurd. They never look at you when they talk. This can be very disconcerting. Their faces seem much more impassive than ours, and they speak without much change in their tone of voice. It is hard to know what they are emphasizing. They seem far more concerned with spatial detail. When Forster told me a few days ago about his experiences in the army, it was only after he had finished what seemed to me at the time to be a long list of places he had been sent to that I realized he had told me he had been deathly ill and had had an affair with a Shoshone girl. In a way he was telling me that he was lonely.

Yesterday, on my way back to Forster's, I passed and tried to comfort a little boy who was wailing in an arbor about a hundred yards from the nearest hogan. A woman looked out of it but did not come over. I walked up to her—she was the mother—and explained that I had heard him crying and had tried to calm him. She listened in silence and then sent a little girl over to fetch him.

JULY 4

As I DID NOT EXPECT FORSTER and his family back until late this evening, I took the opportunity to look through the house and make an inventory. Unfortunately Forster had not given me the keys to his room and the tool shed, but I was able to look through the girls' room and John's.

The girls' room was clearly a teen-agers' room. There was a vanity table, painted pink, covered with cheap cosmetics and a bag of curlers. Cora wears curlers all day long and takes them off at night. Three pictures were Scotch-taped to the mirror: the first, of the girls' half brother, Forster Junior, who is stationed in Germany, in an army uniform; the second, presumably of a boy friend, also in uniform; and the third, of Elvis Presley. There was a large couch, covered with a sheet, which served as a bed; a double bed with a white, slightly soiled chenille bedspread rumpled up in the center; a small bureau, painted pale green; a low white bookcase with a few junior-high English and general math books as well as several odd volumes of the *National Encyclopedia* in it; and a night table piled high with copies of *Romance Comics* and *Look* magazine, to which Forster has a subscription, and a copy of *Good Housekeeping*. Along one wall Forster had improvised a closet out of an old pipe and some slats, and the

girls' clothes—mostly white and checked cotton blouses—
were hanging neatly there. The floor was gray cement.

John's room was little more than two closets juxtaposed
to form a T. There were no windows. It was very dark
and close and smelled of dirty clothes. In the back section
there was only a bar on which a few wrinkled, dirty cowboy shirts were hanging, and in the front a double bunk
frame without mattresses. A sleeping bag was balled up on
the lower bunk, and a pile of scratched 45-rpm records
were spread out over the top one. There was a cheap old
record player on a black wooden chair and to its left an
army footlocker with a bottle of Mennen's after-shave lotion resting on it. It had obviously been forgotten.

My hogan is a fine one as hogans go. They are supposed
to be constructed on the plan of the Navaho cosmos. Mine
has a cement floor, stone walls caked with cement and not
mud, a cedar-beamed roof topped with mud, and a socket
for an electric light which has never been connected with
the power line. It is surprisingly cool, especially in comparison to the clapboard cabins which "civilization" has
brought to the reservation and which are not insulated.

I decided to hike to School House for lunch. I followed
the dirt road, making a rough map and marking every
hogan and arbor on it. I noted the name and clan affiliation of the few camps I had visited and decided to ask
Forster about the others. With the exception of the old
deaf and blind woman who lives in the mud hogan just
east of Forster's, I did not see a single person in the dozen
or so camps I passed. Had everyone in Little Bluff gone to
the Pow-Wow? I wouldn't be surprised—I had seen so
many cars and pickup trucks headed for Flagstaff yesterday morning. There were also a lot of hitchhikers.

On the way back from town, where I had a greasy ham-
burger steak and soggy French fries, I climbed to the top
of the bluff and for the first time got an overview of the
area. Little Bluff is an almost heart-shaped stretch of land,
about five square miles, which is more or less artificially
divided from the low desert plains to the northwest by the
highway that leads to Round Point and Carteret. The
bluff itself, a long ridge of rose-colored sandstone, separates it on the south and east from the highlands where
School House is located. The bluff is deeply eroded and
appears from below as a row of long, wrinkled knuckles.
A little stream trickles down from between the second and
third of these knuckles into a shallow pool that is nearly
dry. I have been told that after a rainstorm water cascades
down the side of the bluff with a roar that you can hear
for miles.

Irrigation ditches radiate out from the pool into the
fields which surround it on three sides. Of these Big
Bead's are the greenest. Indeed they stand in sharp contrast to the cakey red-brown of the other fields, which are
lying fallow because of the drought. Most of the camps are
located, like Forster's, beyond the fields, near the highway.
The Big Bead camp is, again, the exception. It borders on
the pool itself.

JULY 5

FORSTER LOOKED HUNG-OVER. His eyes were
bloodshot, his face sallow and sunken, and his speech
slurred. Lana, John, and Forster had returned late last
night, shortly after midnight, from the Pow-Wow. As they

could not find the key to the kitchen and the girls' bedroom, which I had hidden in the agreed place, Lana slept in the car rather than wake me. She also looked hungover. John was in a grouchy mood.

"The kids not back yet," Forster announced as we were waiting for breakfast. By "kids" he meant his two youngest daughters and the Shepard girls. "I don't know where they are. They run off. Bad kids."

We sat down to a breakfast of scrambled eggs and fried potatoes. No one was much in the mood for eating except me. I was still hungry from my long hike yesterday. As Forster speculated about the whereabouts of the kids—he was clearly worried but not at all panicky the way an American father would have been under those circumstances –Lana remained suspiciously silent. I had the impression that she knew more than she was willing to let on and that, had she not had to return for work, she too would have been missing.

"I spend lot of money at Pow-Wow. Forty dollars," Forster said, changing the subject. He opened his wallet and showed it to me. It was empty. "Flat broke," he said and laughed. "Kids want to ride on anything."

I asked him if he had had much to drink. He said he hadn't, and we all smiled. Forster then announced that he was going to Triple Mountain next weekend and not to Wayne, where Sally works, as he had planned. I asked if Sally was going to be in Triple Mountain.

"Another woman," he answered. "I see Sally at Pow-Wow, but we didn't speak."

We drove John and Lana to work. An attempt was made this summer by the Navaho tribe in conjunction with the federal government to provide as many summer jobs as possible for senior-high-school students. Lana is working as a stenographer and John as a gardener. Forster's vacation, which is to last through July, starts tomorrow.

We parked the car in front of the trading post, where I was going to buy some food, and waited for it to open. Forster asked me where I thought the kids were, and I tried to reassure him. I was in a dilemma. On the one hand, I was curious to see how Forster would handle the situation, and on the other I wanted to urge him to contact the police. Finally I asked him whether he should tell the police. He said nothing.

"I see Sally at Pow-Wow," he said after a few minutes of silence. "We don't speak. On Monday I go to rodeo with woman from Triple Mountain. She good woman. She weaves and takes care of sheep. She's about thirty."

I wanted to know how old Sally was.

"She is twenty-one"; and after a long pause he added, "She no good. Run around too much. She was in jail. Judge give her suspended sentence. She drunk. No good. She jailbird. Other woman, she drive, has driver's license. She driver in Triple Mountain."

A big white station wagon pulled up alongside of us. It was Ralph, a friend of Forster's who had left the reservation fourteen years ago to work in the oil fields in Los Angeles. He had come back with his family to visit relatives. The two friends talked for a while in Navaho, and after Ralph left, Forster told me who he was. He was impressed by Ralph's car and family and wondered whom he had married. "It's difficult to get jobs around here," Forster said. "In California, Ralph ways it pretty easy."

I told him that I thought he had a good job.

"I've been working twenty-eight years. Pretty soon retire, in a year. I get good woman. She weaves. I'll do nothing. Maybe raise some sheep."

We sat in silence. I wondered whether Forster would really be content with such a traditional Navaho life.

The trading post opened. "Sally, she pretty but no good," Forster said as I got out of the car.

The kids were still not back when we returned with the marketing. Forster said he was not feeling well. I went to my hogan to type some notes while he sat under one of the trees and waited. A half hour passed. He knocked at my door.

"Maybe kids can't get ride from Flagstaff," he said. "I go but it long way. I don't have money for gas."

I told him that I had money and would go with him. (He still has not arranged for rent.) He seemed grateful.

On the way to Flagstaff, we looked expectantly into every car we passed. It was hopeless. Most of the cars were going too fast to see anyone besides the driver. Forster said very little. I did learn that he thought Navaho families were too big. We had been discussing Ralph's family, which was small. I asked him about birth-control pills.

"They can get pills from Health Service," he explained. "They take them, but don't know how to use them. Navaho fuck too much."

We stopped for gas. The attendant, an Anglo, spoke excellent Navaho and was Forster's friend. He had not seen the kids but would keep his eye out.

As we approached Flagstaff, Forster pointed out San Francisco Peak, which, he told me, is one of four sacred mountains. He could not remember the names of the others and said that I would have to find out from a medicine man. One thing I am learning is that Forster holds medicine men in great respect. Sometimes I think that he uses the word less to designate someone who is actually a singer than to describe someone he knows and respects who has some knowledge of traditional Navaho lore.*

In Flagstaff we drove around the center of town and then around the fair grounds. A few Indians were helping to dismantle some of the rides, and a few more were fast asleep under trees. Forster pointed out a Papago and told me that the Navaho didn't like them. There was no sign of the girls. We drove back into town and walked around. Forster asked a few Navahos if they had seen the kids, but they hadn't. He seemed very reluctant—embarrassed, I suppose—to go to the police and finally asked me to go. The station was crowded with Indian women who had come to bail out their husbands, most of whom were charged with drunken and disorderly conduct. The police knew nothing of Forster's children.

We drove back to the reservation very discouraged. The return trip seemed much longer. To make matters worse, the transmission—Forster's car has automatic transmission, an absurdity on reservation roads—began to give us trouble as we neared Little Bluff. I didn't think we would make it back. The route, which I had admired on the way, became hot and dusty. We were in the middle of nowhere. We did make it, however. It was nearly dinnertime. The kids were still not home. Forster suggested that perhaps they were at the Shepards' house. I suddenly realized that he had not consulted anybody in the neighborhood, not even someone as obvious as Dan Shepard, the girls' father, about the kids. I offered to walk over and ask. The Shepard house is about half a mile east of Forster's. Like my hogan, it is made of fieldstone but it is unusual in that it is shaped like a small cottage. No one was home.

I began to prepare dinner. "Make anything," Forster

* "Singer" and "medicine man" are used interchangeably for the chief practitioner in a Navaho ceremonial, or sing.

had said. "The kids are gone. I can't eat." He sat very depressed on the terrace in his bent garden chair. He was also worried about the car. At dinner he suddenly began to tell me about the different Navaho clans.

"Many-Goats is named after the people who have many goats," he explained. "Many-Children was named after a man who had many children. He not have one wife. Maybe three. First wife maybe she have ten kids. Second wife, five. Third wife, maybe seven. A lot of kids." Later I checked my list of clans for one called Many-Children, which I had never heard of, and found that there was no such clan. Had Forster been pulling my leg? "The Salt clan is named after people who have plenty of salt. They all have white hair. Even kids have white hair." John, Lana, and Paul, John's friend, all of whom had been listening attentively, smiled. Paul had stopped by with some watermelon from the old blind and deaf woman. Forster was going to take her to a trading post tomorrow.

Forster then talked about Sally again. He was much more talkative than I had ever seen him. Sally, it turns out, is also a daughter of Dan Shepard and the half sister of Joan and Nancy.

"She mad," Forster said. "She saw me at rodeo. I was with Joan. I not speak to her. She very mad. After, I hear she left right away. She not there on second day."

Later, when he complimented me on my cooking, I explained that I had not cooked in a long time because I had a girl friend who did it for me. I told him that maybe I would marry her.

"Don't plan," he said. "Just do at moment. Look at Sally. A man alone has many women. I have four. Sally was first."

After dinner, Forster put on a shocking-pink Robin Hood hat with a baby-blue feather in it. He had bought it at the Pow-Wow. "Joan" was embroidered across the front, and a photograph of Joan Shepard was pinned to it. Forster was obviously upset. At dinner his conversation had jumped abruptly from subject to subject—and now the hat. He hadn't put it on to be funny. Neither Lana, John, nor Paul laughed or even smiled at him. The two boys went into John's room and played a few records; Forster and I talked about the girls and the transmission. He had no plans. Finally I asked him what he would do if the girls did not come back tomorrow. He said he would go to the police, and a few minutes later he decided to go to them right away. We all climbed in the car and chugged our way to Round Point. Forster was about to enter the police station with his pink hat on when I reminded him of it. He took it off embarrassedly. In describing to the police what had happened he consulted me several times about matters I had learned from him. This, I suppose, was to impress the Navaho police sergeant, who took down only the girls' names, thought for a while, and suddenly called Flagstaff by radio. They knew nothing about the girls. He thought some more and finally told us that he would let the patrol cars know. We left.

JULY 6

WHILE WAITING FOR LANA to make breakfast, Forster presented me with his plan for repairing the transmission. The problem was simple: he has no money and will not have any for a week, until payday; he will try to establish credit at one of the local garages. We sat down to breakfast. Forster asked Lana whether the girls were going to eat. I looked up in surprise.

"Kids, they come back late, so late," he explained matter-of-factly. "Bad kids."

I asked him where they had been and what had happened, but he dismissed my questions with a gesture showing he wasn't interested. He either did not know or did not want to tell me. I don't think he really knew. All I could learn was that a friend from town had given them a ride back to the reservation.

The radio, which constantly blares out five-minute news reports, pop music, and friendly finance advertisements, announced that a Navaho, Red Julius, had been murdered at the Pow-Wow. A carload of Papagos had also been killed in an accident. Forster made no comment; he didn't know the Navaho.

Forster drove John and Lana to work and returned about an hour later. He had evidently not been able to obtain credit and was disturbed both because he would not be able to take the old woman to the trading post and because he would probably not be able to go to Triple Mountain.

"Maybe my son Douglas, one in Window Rock, come," he said. "We go to Carteret and then to Grand Canyon to see Rita. She work in restaurant. Just graduate from school."

The Reeds live in an unsheltered camp in the middle of a cornfield. According to Gene, they are one of the poorest families in Little Bluff. Joe Reed, who is married to a neighbor's eldest daughter, Mary, is a farmer and has thirteen children. He and his fifteen-year-old son, Tim, were rebuilding a wagon out of bits and pieces of other wagons, which were scattered in front of their hogan, when I arrived at eleven this morning. Joe greeted me in Navaho and listened attentively as I explained my purpose. Tim translated. He told me that he was busy now but might have time to talk to me later. When I offered to help, Joe said nothing, but went back to work. I stood around and watched for a long time before I found an opportunity to help. They accepted this without comment. I was astonished at their ingenuity. Not only were they putting together a wagon out of what seemed to me to be a hopeless mess of parts but they had almost no tools. Joe would cut a metal bar by grooving all four sides with an old ax head and then hammering it off. He worked rapidly in the hot sun, which he did not seem to mind, and would occasionally hum or sing. He was the first Navaho I had heard sing. His voice was nasal, and he sang in what was probably Spanish. I could not be sure. Joe ignored me almost completely, but Tim seemed curious and would ask me questions from time to time about where I was from and how I had come to the reservation.

While we were working, a bus filled with white children drove up to Mary's mother's camp, which is about a hundred yards away. Everyone turned to look. I asked Tim who they were.

"Bus from Gallup," he said. "They come last year. They come to look around."

I wish I could describe the expression on his face as he stared at the white children in the distance. It was one of envy and bitterness, shame and pride. Mary Reed with several of her children walked over to her mother's camp, and when she returned after the bus had left, Joe and Tim joined her under the arbor. They whispered among themselves for a few minutes and then returned to work. Tim was chewing gum. Under the supervision of their teacher, the white children had given the Navaho ones candy and gum.

We continued to rebuild the wagon. Tim asked me

when I was going and then suggested I ask any questions I
might have now. It was apparent that they wanted me to
go because they were preparing lunch and were too poor
to offer me any. I stopped working and asked Mary Reed a
few questions, more for the sake of formality than for information. At first Mary did not want to answer any of my
questions, but as soon as she learned why and how I had
come, and that I was "a Christian"—Mary belongs to the
Assembly of God—she became cooperative. She asked me
if I had a car. The whole family seems very concerned
about transportation. I suppose they have a very hard
time getting around. She was very reluctant to talk about
farming. I did learn, however, that they have some sheep
in the mountains, which are tended by two of her sons,
and that Joe does not help any of the other people in Little Bluff.

Today is officially the first day of Forster's vacation. He
has nothing to do and feels trapped because of his car
trouble. He spent the day cleaning the house and car and
fixing the latrine door. He has one of the few latrines in
Little Bluff. Most of the Navahos relieve themselves in
open but well-hidden places—they are very modest—and
bury their feces. Traditionally they feared they could be
used against them by witches.

Forster does not seem to be able to get Sally out of his
mind. He talked about her both before and after dinner.

"Kids see Sally. Her face all scarred," he said with dis-
gust. "She say two women jumped her. She in hospital
eight days. I don't believe. I think men did it. She runs
around too much. So do her sisters." Her sisters would include Joan, I thought to myself. "She even leave school in
town, graduate from another school, because she get laid
too much."

Forster believes that her parents sent her off-reservation to work to keep her out of trouble.

"She earns forty dollars a week and lives in building where she says she has to be back at eleven clock at night. We go Albuquerque one day. Sally she drive in city. I don't like to drive in city because too many cars and one-way streets. We go to matinée and get back to her place at ten thirty. I spend night there."

Forster is supposed to marry her—at least, so he claims. She has left clothes and pictures at his place.

"I give her plenty clothes. Over one hundred dollars' worth. Give her watch when she graduate from school and suit last Christmas. It cost forty dollars. She no good. She run round too much."

He complained about the Pow-Wow. He was sorry he had gone. "It was dirty." When I asked him why girls run around so much, he answered hesitantly, "I don't know. They're crazy. They think they're pretty or something." I don't think he had ever thought about it before.

I wanted to know about Sally's family.

"Dan, he drink too much," Forster answered. "Her mother work on sheep camp. Maybe Sally she not want to see me. She embarrassed to see me because face all scarred. Ugly."

His conversation continued along these lines, but as the evening progressed, Sally grew worse and worse—she even bleached her hair—though she always remained pretty. I felt sorry for Forster. He seemed obsessed with her. What struck me as interesting was the extent to which he would let his imagination go, often in direct contradiction to an early fantasy. His concern about her scarred face seemed more symbolic than real. The fight which she had been in had occurred over a month ago, and Forster himself had seen her at the Pow-Wow and had made no mention of her scars until today. Sally's dilemma seemed more understandable. Torn between *Romance Comics* and a more or less traditional marriage, she had nothing to do but have a fling. Before going to bed, Forster asked me not to mention Sally to Dan Shepard if I should see him.

JULY 7

AT BREAKFAST:

"I dream of Sally," Forster said, with what appeared to me to be a touch of embarrassment, "because we talk about her."

"What was the dream?" I asked, after a long silence.

"Crazy dream . . . I wasn't married then . . ." and then changing the subject he added, "There is an old-age home in Wayne. I took some people there last week. Only Negroes work there. They nicer than Navaho. Navaho don't care for old people." Wayne is where Sally works.

Forster has asked me for the second time whether I had seen Harold Kennedy. From time to time, as he sits in front of the house he peers in the direction of Harold's cabin, barely visible in the distance, and mumbles something or other about Harold's absence. It is confusing.

The rains are late and the fields crusty. The wind is always blowing up a dust storm. (My nose is stuffed and my ears plugged with red sand.) The predominant color is red, but when the sun sets, the bluff takes on all the possible hues between scarlet and gray-blue.

There are about fifteen families here now—sometimes

more. They are all large—eight, ten, twelve children
(thanks to the Public Health Service) and incomes are
small. The people eke out a living from the dried-up
fields, welfare, and wage work in School House. I'm only a
few miles away from this metropolis, and were anything
going on here I'd write a book and call it *Navaho Subur-
bia*. But that's just the problem. Little Bluff is boring.
Very little ever happens: no peyote meetings (the police
are too close), no ceremonials (summer is not the ceremonial season), no farming (the fields are too dry).

Forster is comparatively wealthy. He earns about ninety
dollars a week. He's been married four times and has
eight children in all. His girls—the ones I know—are especially shy. When they see me they run in the opposite
direction. They've never really spoken to me. Even John
doesn't speak to me much, but I think this is out of resentment. I'm a little like an older brother who has monopolized his father's time, if not affection.

The big drama in the household is whether or not Forster will marry Sally. She's more than twenty years younger
than he, and, from what I can gather, a real bitch. He's
asked for it though. He plays the sugar daddy. I really like
him and feel sorry for him. He's tied down to the house
now and spends all his time thinking about her. It's sort
of pathetic. . . .

JULY 8

Rita came home late last night. I caught
only a glimpse of her. She is homely and not at all as so-
phisticated-looking as Lana.

This morning I brought up the subject of witchcraft. A VISTA worker had been accused of being a witch. I was a little reticent because I had heard that the Navahos do not like to discuss witchcraft, but I was very curious to see Forster's reaction. Gene had told me that it is still a very live issue. He had seen the movie *Bell, Book, and Candle* in a Navaho theater a few years ago and was surprised at how quiet the audience had become during the witch scenes. Usually the auditorium is so noisy—the Navaho talk throughout a showing—that you can't hear a thing.

"People, they call some people witches," Forster explained. "They call Tall Singer a witch."

I asked why.

"Because he medicine man."

When I asked about Old Man Big Bead, Forster laughed, and after a pause, "Sometimes him too." I wanted to know about several other older men in the area, but Forster ignored my questions. He seemed lost in thought. Finally when I tried to find out whether a white doctor could be a witch, he woke from his revery.

"No, white men cannot be witches."

"And Hopi?"

"Yes, Hopi, they are witches."

I wanted to know what witches do.

"Maybe they kill people. It is illegal. They go to jail. Maybe they fined two hundred dollars, if they kill someone. Go to jail, just like if they take peyote."

"How do you know if someone is a witch?"

"They say it. Maybe hand shaker find out. They can know. They can find out everything." He was referring to Navaho seers whose arms, covered with corn pollen, tremble as they perform their divination.

"My sisters and my mother's sister, they are very rich," he said, changing the subject. "They have many sheep. Sally and me, we go there. My mother's sister, she give Sally a big fat sheep. Sally say we get married for sure. Why does she run round? Now they don't like her. She no good." I wonder if Forster's sisters and his mother's sister have ever been accused of witchcraft. Wealthy Navahos are often accused of it; this would explain his train of thought. I am probably going too far.

Before lunch I asked Forster to tell me about his life. He seemed pleased at my interest and at the same time reluctant. Finally he began.

"I don't know where I was born. I don't know exactly my birthday, because I didn't see my mother and father. They died when I was a baby. I think in 1918. A lot of people die on reservation then. Big flu or something. That was the time they die. I was raised by my grandmother [mother's mother]. I don't even know her name. It was around High Point. My father, he come from around Red Mountain. She have sheep and livestock. Plenty livestock.

"And then I went to school. Here in town first: 1927, I think. And then to Fort Apache after 1927. Until 1930. From 1930 until 1934 I went to school at Fort Wingate, New Mexico. And then in 1936 start working in town. It was for CCC—not government. I get married in 1936— that was my second wife—until 1942. My first wife, married only one year. I got divorced. Then in 1942 I get another wife. This belong to these kids. She my wife until 1954. She was killed in accident in 1954. Her name was Laura. Automobile accident on road from Gallup.

"I start on school job in 1939. I work in same place today. Same job, maintenance man. From 1942 to 1945 I was in the United States Army. From 1945 to 1948 I was working at an army depot. From 1948 until now I work at school."

Forster stopped. I waited for him to continue, but he said nothing. Finally I asked him what it was like when he was young.

"I was home. Sheepherder. Help at home like these kids. That was before I go to school. My grandmother died in 1956."

I wanted to know what he thought of school.

"Just went to school. I don't think I like school. It long time ago. I don't remember."

I asked him more about the army.

"I go to basic training in Texas. It was six weeks. I was the only Navaho. I guess some other places there were Navaho. There were some other Indians, Spanish, Germans, all kinds. Then I was in Pennsylvania after that in army base. I came back to Texas after six months' training with other soldiers. I was at POE [port of embarkation] station, that is, where they ship them across ocean. I came back in 1943 to Texas, to different place. I was stationed there for a little while and then shipped to Seattle, Washington. And then we went to Aleutian Islands in '44. I was just there one month and came back to Seattle. Then they shipped us to Hawaii and some other islands, to Okinawa. I was in Okinawa in 1945. The war was over, and I came for discharge with sixty-nine points [priority rating]. Then I come to Hawaii in 45 to rest camp. Stayed there twenty days for transportation. Then finally to San Peter [San Pedro?], California. I got discharged December 3, 1945, at Fort McArthur, California. The next day I just came home. I was not working for a month and then I started to at army depot."

We had to stop for lunch. I was struck by the way Forster had divided his life almost mechanically into socially defined periods of time. He did not consider it important to fill in these periods with memories of specific events or feelings. How much of this has to do with what he thought I wanted to know and how much of it is a fair representation of how he conceives of his past I cannot determine.

Forster again asked me whether I had seen Harold Kennedy. It appears that he has been missing since the Pow-Wow. Forster's only comment was, "He not around; he plenty drunk at Pow-Wow."

After lunch I visited Tall Singer. I had noticed that Willy Murphy was back—he had not been around for a few days—and hoped that he would translate for me. Willy was reluctant even after a promise of more cigarettes. He said his "brother" was old and had been asked questions by a white man who showed him pictures a few weeks ago. Tall Singer seemed senile but talkative. Willy proved a terrible translator. He would doze off as the medicine man talked and then condense a five-minute speech into a sentence or two.

Tall Singer was crouching on a sheepskin rug. He was dressed in baggy gray trousers and a wrinkled blue work shirt. Long turquoise earrings dangled from his ears. They were bigger than Big Bead's, but Tall Singer's necklace was less impressive. His hair was knotted tightly with white cord. His cheekbones were higher and sharper than those of most Navahos, his nose larger and more angular, and his eyes were very dark, beady. He was chewing tobacco and would spit from time to time into a rusty coffee can. Yellow spittle had dried on his few whiskers.

Two women in traditional dress, one in her early fifties, the other much older, whom I had seen several times before under a brush arbor nearby, were preparing dough for fried bread, which, much to my surprise, they put in popover tins and then into the Franklin stove. Occasionally the women would blow their noses into their hands or spit on the floor. Toward the end of the interview, two boys, Tall Singer's grandchildren, came in for lunch. They were dressed in dusty blue jeans and dirty polo shirts.

Willy's rough translation of Tall Singer's speech: "This old man here, he is medicine man. He puts out prayers for different families. He helps many people. . . . There are different prayers just like different denominations. I don't know much about these things. He has used his ceremonies to cure his wife and this woman here." Willy pointed to the younger woman. "That is why she is here now. She helps him because he has helped her. . . . He has eleven grandchildren. His fields are dry, but he supports his entire family, even his grandchildren. That is much work, but he does it. A few days ago he was asked questions by someone who showed him pictures. He answer questions and now he is tired." I had the impression that it was Willy, and not Tall Singer, who was tired. "He knows many things. There is a ceremony that he knows. It is called Beauty Way [actually *hojonji,* or Blessing Way]. I think that is how you white men call it. Beauty Way is like a prayer. When there is sickness he would say it over them. It is their way. . . . I don't know much about these things. It is a religion so many hundred years old. He learned it from his father. He has followed his father's footsteps. . . . They learn it when first people taught Navaho many things—Holy People who help Navaho. He knows many of these things . . . He has helped many people. White men do not know these things, but he does. He is old now and. . . ."

Willy was getting very tired. Tall Singer continued talking, but Willy was unable to translate. I listened as the old man spoke. I was very impressed by the quality of his voice—its lulling effect—and the way he pointed with his long, thin fingers and motioned with his hands, which, palms down and paralleling the ground, followed the contour of his speech. I tried to arouse Willy but without success. Tall Singer did not seem to care whether Willy was translating or not. Finally he took his social security card out of his wallet and showed it to me.

"He wants you to know his name," Willy said at last. "He has two sons and four daughters. Now he wants to eat."

"I come from Pittsburgh by train when I was in army," Forster reminisced before dinner. "It take three days. Cost fifty dollars—fifty-one dollars and fifty cents. Fifty-one fifty not to here but to Carteret. Some civilians I seen, they stand all the way. There was MP there. He say all military personnel go on first." Forster laughed. "I sit all the way. There were some women, they have to stand. Soldiers sit.

"Then we have training in Hawaii. I was sergeant. I made marksman. We fired all kinds of guns: pistols, M-1, machine guns, all kind guns. Sometimes five rounds, sometimes ten. One whole week, nothing but firing. Machine guns hardest. They make you a little deaf. I usually put something in my ears. When we finished, I thought we go for more training, but then it was war."

"That must have been terrible," I said sympathetically.

"We fight," he continued in monotone. "I was wounded. Not shot. Something hit and piece flies at me. I was reported missing in action in paper. Maybe I have paper here. I show you. I was in military hospital, but before that I wait under tree for long time. There were so many of us, just like ants." He pointed to some red ants, which were crawling on the terrace. "It was hard. Sometimes we had to go on scouting mission. I went for two days. We crawl through jungle. And there we see machine gun. Just as far as that pole." He pointed to an electric-wire post about twenty-five yards away. "Maybe a hundred yards. There was Japanese colonel. I seen him talking. I had radio. I call back CP and speak in Navaho. They send more men. Later I see place. Just nothing there. They capture colonel, and put him in charge of prisoners. He had no KP. Just in charge."

The girls called us to dinner. Forster continued his narration.

"There was picture of me jumping from boat. Water so high." He pointed to his chest. "And we had to run crooked. If they fire, we have to hit ground. The first night we have to build foxhole. Gun, knife, and foxhole are our best friends."

"Food!" John interrupted. Forster hadn't touched a thing. I had never seen him so involved in what he was talking about. It was almost compulsive.

"Sometimes buddy they help. Everywhere we go we take gun. In case somebody jump us, we have gun. We crawl with gun. Sometimes we stay in foxhole for three days. We kill everything. I see birds. They get killed. Machine guns drop them from trees. Nothing left on island. All killed. Horses. Everything. It smell just like meat not in refrigerator. Everything rotten. . . ." Forster grimaced.

"Then I come back. First to San Peter. Boat docks, there train. But first a line of two hundred for doughnuts and coffee. Red Cross. Band played and played. Colonel he speaks to us before we leave Hawaii and asks for volunteers to stay in army. They would make me staff sergeant.

Nobody volunteer. I guess maybe somebody volunteer. Then we get on train and then we go to place in California for discharge. I don't remember name. There was big mountain there. It was near Los Angeles. I call my wife. These kids were not there yet, not even Kitty. They not know World War II. My wife she come. It was Friday. It was terrible when we arrive. No discharge until Monday. Too many people on Monday. I discharged on Tuesday afternoon. They give me fifty dollars in cash and a check. A lot of money. Almost fifteen hundred dollars. My wife she work in hospital. She save money from state. I stay in Gallup. No job. I go to depot. They give me job in three days. My wife she quit work to come stay with me. We couldn't get car then. We went to Albuquerque. Bought used Mercury. Big car. Pay nine hundred dollars for it."

Forster stopped to eat. Dinner consisted of a sort of stew made with two cans of Campbell's chicken noodle soup, a quarter of a pound of margarine, and enough sliced potatoes to feed five. This and fried chicken necks have been our staple for the last few days.

"I go to New York City when I in army," Forster said, suddenly. I looked up, amazed. Considering the questions he had asked me about New York, I couldn't believe my ears. "I was in army in Pennsylvania. I had weekend pass. There was street there called Washington Street with big bridge. I went to U.S.O. I had big steak dinner for fifty cents. At night they took money at desk. They were right with all kinds of soldiers there. Yes. Next day sergeant come. He brought me there. He had car. He takes me home to place, long way, Brook . . . I forget name. Brooklyn. Yes, that right, Brooklyn. And we eat long noodles, real long noodles, so long." Forster stretched his hands as wide as he could. "So long," he said, and all the children laughed. "I forget name."

"You mean spaghetti."

"Yes, that right, spaghetti. I like them, very good, except too difficult to eat. They were with chili sauce."

Forster refers to any red or hot sauce as chili sauce. He prides himself on how hot a sauce he can eat. Once he added so much tabasco sauce to his chopped meat and canned-stringbean soup that he could hardly eat it. He has told me that it is good for your virility.

I asked him how he liked New York City.

"Big. Many cars. Everything over my eyes."

I promised to make Forster and his family some spaghetti. They are now using instant coffee, which I mistakenly bought, instead of regular coffee, which they had always overcooked. They now prefer the instant.

Just as we finished dinner, Harold Kennedy walked in. He was wearing khaki trousers and a white dress shirt. His face was drawn and anxious. His eyes were watery and sad. Forster seemed relieved to see him. Harold had been in jail all this time. He had been drunk during the Pow-Wow and was very upset because the police had taken his fingerprints. They suspected him of the murder of Red Julius, the Navaho who had been found slain near a trading post during the Pow-Wow. Harold had been picked up in the same general area.

JULY 9

AT BREAKFAST I TOLD FORSTER that Gene had asked me to go with him to a Hopi long-haired kachina dance.*

* This is one of a long cycle of Hopi ceremonials held from December through July and August in which members of a special

"Navaho and Hopi, they not very friendly," Forster replied. "You not see any Navaho there. The Hopi try to take Navaho land. If Hopi and Navaho friendly, you see all kind Navaho there.

"Hopi make good bread and tamales," he continued after a pause. "Not like this bread." He pointed to a loaf of commercial sandwich bread. "Sweet. Maybe you bring some back. Navaho bread good too. These kids know how to make but lazy. Lazy kids. Maybe they make some one these days."

After breakfast, as Forster and I were watering his trees —it is so dry that they need to be watered every day now —a white Ford pickup truck drove up. It was Larry, who, Forster explained, knows a lot about cars.

"This man, he and his uncle have big collection all kinds parts of cars. You see his garage. All full of parts: valves, gas pumps, distributors, spark plugs, carburetors, all kinds accessories and parts. Maybe even transmission for this car."

Forster has not yet been able to have his car fixed. Payday is still three days off.

"He student," Forster said, introducing me to Larry "Come all way from New York. He study Navaho people. He live here in that hogan there. Just like Navaho. Ask plenty questions. Maybe he ask you some. Tell him name." Forster turned to me. He could not pronounce my name.

The two men began to talk, half in Navaho, half in English, about the transmission. Larry had heard about Forster's problem and had stopped by to see what he could do. Forster explained what was wrong with the car,

---

ceremonial fraternity impersonate spirits known as kachina in both private and public performances. The spirits are also given material form in the kachina dolls for which the Hopi are well known.

and Larry agreed that it must be the transmission. Both men stood around the car in silence.

"He go to Hopi dance today," Forster broke the silence. "I tell him Hopi no good. They try to take Navaho land. . . . Anybody can make kachina [doll]. They come from root of tree. They hand-made, not *technologically* made. . . . Maybe you bring back Hopi woman."

Both men laughed. "I have transmission," Larry said. "Maybe it fit. Maybe not."

Forster and Larry stood in thought.

"You have here?" Forster asked finally.

The transmission, which came from an old Mercury, was at Larry's uncle's in town. Both men drove off to get it and returned within a half hour. Forster removed it from the truck, single-handed. John was told to crawl under the car and compare the two transmissions. He did not think they were the same; they had different numbers.

"They change transmission every so often," Forster said. "Maybe eight years, maybe ten years. In 1949 there was new model and in 1959."

"No, they change model in 1956," Larry asserted.

"No, they change it every ten years. In 1955 and then in 1965."

"And then maybe in 1975."

The two men finally agreed upon a ten-year interval beginning in the middle of the decade. Then they asked me whether I thought the transmissions were the same. I didn't think so.

"You learn much about Navaho?" Larry asked.

I told him I was.

"You learn language?"

I explained that I was trying but that it was very difficult. Larry asserted that Navaho was an easy language—not like English—and proceeded to teach me a few words:

the word for screwdriver, because he happened to be holding one in his hand, and then the word for fingernail. He showed me one of his fingernails which had been split by a shovel when he was a child and had never healed. His uncle, with whom he had been living—both his parents had died about the time he was born—had made him work very hard.

Forster and Larry finally decided that the transmissions were not the same and drove back to town to call Carteret, where, it turned out, Forster had made a down payment on a used transmission a few months ago. They soon returned. The telephone lines were out of order. Forster made a few more deprecatory remarks about the Hopi and then told me that he would have joined Gene and me at the dance had he not been expecting his son Douglas. Did he feel left out?

Larry asked me again what I was learning about the Navaho and then if I had heard anything about peyote. I told him I hadn't, and Forster immediately assured me that they both were against it. Larry did not seem to me to be against it, but both men denied having ever taken it. I was told that both Don Alexander and Robert Arthur, the two candidates for the tribal chairmanship, were against it, but that peyote takers were generally in favor of Arthur, the New Guard representative, who was more sympathetic to their cause. Gene later explained that much of Navaho politics was cleaved along the lines of the candidate's unofficial stand on peyote.

"I take you to peyote meeting before end of vacation on August 1," Forster promised, much to my surprise. "I help you. I find all about it."

At first I attributed this offer to Forster's desire to impress Larry with his willingness to help me, but on further consideration I decided that he also wanted to help me out of friendship and that he probably wanted to learn more about peyote himself. I sometimes feel that my analyses of his motivation are too mechanical.

The two men were trying to decide where peyote came from, and after much speculation in a mixture of English and Navaho, which I could not follow, they decided it "was shipped from Texas and Mexico by airmail."

Gene arrived, and we left for the dance. The ride was long, hot, and beautiful, almost too beautiful. One minute I felt exalted by the beauty of the area and the next bored. My eyes seemed to tire of the expanse. Looking was work. Gene was right. You had to put much more into your perception here. Whenever I let my eyes relax, the surroundings seemed to pass by like a movie out of focus.

There was a subtle change in the countryside as we approached the Hopi villages. It was softer, quieter, easier to take in. Red had given way to tan. It reminded me a little of southern Italy—views I had once had of the Apennines from a train to Sicily. Some of the rock formations looked like ruins. I felt more at home.

This "feeling at home" has troubled me. There has been something very disconcerting about living with the Navaho. Perhaps it is their organization of space. There are no centers. Camps are scattered across the territory in a pattern, if there is a pattern, which is very different from ours, which is dominated by centers—villages, towns, cities. Navaho centers are more or less artificial and often seem to be products of the white man's world: a trading post, a school, a mine. All this became clear to me only when I entered the Hopi village, a thick cluster around which the rest of their space is organized. It looked a little like a medieval mountain town, with its surrounding fields. Obviously this spatial difference I felt can be explained in terms of the difference in the economies of the two tribes: the Navaho are sheepherders and the Hopi farmers. Still, I wonder to what extent this contrast in spatial organization on a demographic level also occurs on a perceptual one.

At the beginning of the trip I was anxious to talk to Gene about my experiences—to get some perspective—but I soon tired of talking. I do not know whether it was the effect of the drive or something else—frustration perhaps at discovering that Forster had been in New York and at how little he seemed to have absorbed, especially in light of questions he had asked me about canyons and sheepherding in the city. Gene told me that he had once taken several old Navahos to San Francisco and that as they approached the city he could almost see a curtain fall across their eyes. It was too much for them to take in. I thought of Forster's expression: "Everything was over my eyes."

The dance itself had an almost hypnotic effect upon me. I listened to the droning voices and rattles of the long-haired, masked dancers, occasionally interrupted by the voice of their Hopi leader (the men who are impersonating the kachina spirits are led by a human guide), and was carried away by the slow, often monotonous movement of the line of dancers. From time to time I would watch the expressions on the round faces of the Hopi children as they peered wonderingly at the dancers, waiting for the gifts—dolls, baskets, oranges, husks of corn, bows and arrows—the spirits had brought for them. Off to the side I could see the village toughs, dressed in tight black jeans and pointed shoes or boots, smugly watching the dance. The majority of the Hopis were dressed neatly in their best clothes. The women were wearing short skirts and blouses and were seated on stools and benches around the edge of the dance square and on the roofs overlooking it. The men stood mostly against the walls of the houses and on the rooftops. In one corner I could see Don Talayesva, the author of *Sun Chief*. I had no idea he was still alive. Here and there I saw white men and even a few Navahos. Forster had been wrong.

After the dance we drove to a nearby trading post for something to eat. It was closed, but a family of San Domingo Pueblos who had not been able to sell all their homemade bread at a rodeo sold us some sweet rolls they had baked in their earthen ovens. They were delicious, and I bought some extra to take back for Forster and the children.

As we were about to leave, a Navaho truck pulled into the one remaining parking place just before a white man did. The Navahos had not cut him off, but he claimed they did, screamed at them furiously, and parked his car in such a way that they could not get out. They watched him without a word. We stayed to see what would happen. He walked off to a nearby garage, gossiped with the owner, and five minutes later returned to his car, which he then locked. Gene and I walked over and asked him what he thought he was doing.

"Did you see what these dirty sons-of-bitches did?" he asked. "The bastards cut me off. I'm going to teach them a lesson."

The Navahos looked on silently. We told him that he had better move the car.

"It's clear, you don't know Indians," he yelled. "They're no-good bastards, lazy bastards. They don't do a god damn thing. They just collect welfare checks. That's all they're good for. I know. I've lived on reservations twenty-five years, I know the sons-of-bitches."

He jumped into his car and drove off. Gene and I returned to ours and left. The Navaho family watched us leave. They never said a word.

JULY 10

AT BREAKFAST Forster did not seem very interested in hearing about the Hopi dance and ate none of the bread I had brought, although his children did. He had spent yesterday with the Gardners, who live near Harold Kennedy, and had watched them put in a new crankshaft; they had raised the car by ropes attached to a tree. Later Harold served a big meal of freshly slaughtered mutton and gave Forster some extra meat to take home. In the evening they went to a dance at Round Point. (Later I found a bottle of muscatel in the garbage can.) Forster seemed to be telling me, "Look how much you missed by going to the katchina dance." His son Douglas never came.

Forster was once a Baptist and is now a Presbyterian. Gene told me that when his third wife died in 1954 he devoted considerable effort to church activities. Now he seldom goes to church.

At lunch Forster suddenly announced that he had stood within two feet of General MacArthur in Okinawa in 1944 and tried to salute, but the general wouldn't let him. Forster asked me why the general had been fired and then told me about a colonel married to a Chinese woman he had known in Hawaii.

"He had plenty hard time. Many soldiers marry Japanese girls. They pretty for a while and then they get old and ugly. Hawaiians pretty just like Mexicans. Not Hopi, they get fat pretty easy, just like Spanish."

"I have to go and wash"—Forster excused himself a few minutes later. This is his euphemism for going to the outhouse. While John was cleaning the latrine this morning, he had found a spider in it which he had not been able to kill. This had caused a great deal of excitement.

When Forster returned, he asked me to come with him to a local chapter meeting in School House, which was scheduled for one o'clock. "They meet every other week," he explained. "They hear reports and talk about Navaho business. Reports from Navaho Tribal Council. Today Paul Harper talk against trader. I see him yesterday at dance. He tell me that the trader is no good. He charges too much. Potatoes cost three times more than in Carteret."

I had, in fact, been astonished at the markup on food at the trading post.

The chapter meeting lasted four hours. It was conducted entirely in Navaho along standard American procedural lines except for elections. Two were held: one for election registrar—Navaho tribal elections are to be held in November—and the other for a preschool bus driver. After the candidates had been nominated, they each stood in a separate corner surrounded by their supporters. A count was then taken. The whole procedure seemed somewhat clumsy and embarrassing. There was a lot of hesitation, and several people did not vote. They obviously did not wish to risk offending one candidate by supporting another. The expressions of both winners were completely impassive.

I was impressed by the attention span of the audience.

There were eighty-seven people present, including two or three babies. Nearly all of them were from town, and almost half of them were women, mostly dressed in traditional costume. There were only three people from Little Bluff present. Although many of the speeches were long and drawn-out, especially the one made by Paul Harper, who never did get in his complaints about the trader, there was almost no talking and shuffling of feet. The people sat in silence, seldom looking around, and listened attentively until nearly the end of the meeting when they began to grow restless.

Aside from the elections, business included a detailed outline of election procedures, a report from the Tribal Council representative (who looked like a Navaho Thomas E. Dewey) concerned with budgetary matters and the failure of the tribe to sign a contract with a factory—the one where Sally works, which Forster fears will fall into Hopi hands—discussions of a federal housing project, and news of a legal-aid service program.

Forster tried to get me to speak. He argued that the Navaho had been nice to me and were curious about me—they even mentioned me in the minutes!—and would like to hear from me. He walked to the front of the room, beckoned the president over, and told him his idea. Fortunately for me—I had no desire to speak—the president informed him that there was no time today but there would be at the next meeting. Forster, who was clearly politicking, returned crestfallen just as a tall, husky Navaho, whom I had noticed because of his dramatic bearing, took the floor.

The speaker's effect was magnetic. The room became silent and all eyes were turned to him. He spoke in a deep, warm voice for about twenty minutes. Occasionally the audience would break into laughter, but most of the time they were dead serious. Forster would turn to me from time to time and nod in agreement.

"Good speech," he said when it was finished. "I tell you after."

The meeting lasted for a few more minutes. A man asked for help because he had no water for his sheep, but the chapter could not help him because he was out of their jurisdiction. There was some laughter.

After the meeting, Forster tried to find out more about the housing program, whereby it is possible to get a tiled house with running water for payments of fifteen dollars a month for twenty-five years. He seemed interested in signing up until I pointed out that his house was better than the ones offered and that for that amount of money he could install sinks, a shower, and a stove.

On the way back, Forster paraphrased the tall, husky Navaho's speech. "He say government try to fight poverty. Navaho ought to fight poverty, but he didn't think we could. In the beginning there was Life, and Life wanted to kill Poverty. Poverty said that if it killed, Life would have nothing to do. So man spared Poverty. And it exist today. It keeps man occupied. There is alcohol and poverty and peyote and they keep things turning. They will never be killed." "Alcohol" and "peyote" may have been Forster's additions.

Later I discovered in Gladys Reichard's *Navaho Religion* that Monster Slayer, one of the legendary Navaho Hero Twins, spared Poverty in his campaign against the monsters who inhabited the earth.

If we did not exist [Poverty argued], people would always have to wear the same clothes and would never get anything new. If we live, things will wear out and people will make beautiful new garments; they will have possessions and look nice. Let us live to pull their clothes to pieces for them.

When we returned to Little Bluff, we walked over the ridge behind Forster's house to inspect his cornfield, which is about four acres. This year has been so dry that only a few plants have survived. One of the Big Bead boys did the plowing for Forster for thirty-five dollars.

Before dinner Forster told me more of his military experiences. His motivation for telling me about his army life interests me. At first I attributed it to a desire to bridge our different worlds. The army was obviously the most intense experience he had ever shared with white men, if not the most intense experience in his life. Now I am beginning to realize that his motivation is much more complex. His constant reference to it seems to indicate a need for catharsis.

While he was in the military hospital in Pennsylvania, presumably suffering from pneumonia, his company commander visited him to tell him that his outfit had been ordered to Europe without him and that "he was a lucky son-of-bitch." When he recovered he was stationed at the hospital for three months as a surgical assistant.

"It was easiest time I had in army. Only drill in morning and sometimes at night. Otherwise it was just work."

He was then sent to Texas to an artillery outfit and after three months to Seattle, the Aleutian Islands, and Hawaii, as he had told me before. This time he went through all the islands in the Pacific on which he had fought: Midway, Saipan, and Guadalcanal. The latter turned out to be the island where he served as a scout.

"It was worst I ever seen. I seen the American. They cut his throat, his nose, his tongue, and his ears right off. They slit his neck. Then Japanese leave him for everybody to see. We fought like hell. They tried to capture a hill, which was surrounded by a tunnel filled with ammunition. Then they relieved us with fifteen thousand troops. Gosh, the smell. All dead bodies. First time I try to eat but couldn't. Second time I could eat everything. They capture plenty prisoners. We pulled them out—the Japanese—like jack rabbits. I mean cottontails. I was sergeant then. They dug hole and lined prisoners there in front of it. Then they shoot them. The prisoners fall into hole and bulldozer comes and pushes dirt over them. Gosh, we was mad. Only time we was mad. The Japanese didn't think Americans fight. They think Americans scared by dead soldier they sent back. Gosh, no tongue, no ears. Freddy Big Bead was supposed to be there. He seen American soldier too.

"I have friend there. We was in foxhole. He was about two, three feet away from me. We talked and didn't know there was machine gun on top of us. We talked and then he was shot with machine gun. I didn't even know. I saw his tongue sticking out. Just like this." Forster stuck his tongue out. "He was a German. He said he had been two feet from Hitler. He was last to escape from Germany. He got American citizenship right away. He work in motel, maybe hotel, in New York. Big tall building. And then they drafted him, and he killed for Americans. He didn't go to Germany. I don't know how I was saved. Some people have luck. Some people no luck. That morning I prayed. I had to. He saw me and he call out, 'Crazy Indian, what you doin'?' I put Red Cross flag on him and stretcher-bearers come right away. They even shoot stretcher-bearers and they not suppose to. It was terrible. I have picture of him somewhere. I don't know where.

"There was another guy," Forster continued after a long pause. "I never forget him. He took bayonet, and every time he see dead Japanese, he opens mouth and knocks out gold tooth with bayonet." Forster laughed. "I never forget him. He was funny guy. When we get to Okinawa we were not allowed to take things—gold teeth and watches. Only in Guadalcanal. We was so mad."

At dinner Forster asked me whether "United States still ruled Japan." He seemed confused and disappointed to hear that we didn't.

"Okinawa most beautiful place I ever seen. There was no villages. Maybe now villages. I get letter from my wife every two weeks. She was nurse. The day we beat Japanese, the whistles blow in town. Everybody went out and dance. Big Squaw Dance. Any kind of dance. Nobody had to work next day."

The Squaw Dance, also known as Enemy Way, is a ceremonial which is designed to kill the ghost of an enemy who is haunting a Navaho and which many Navaho veterans had when they returned from World War II. Forster claims he has never had the ceremony.

"Where you go in army?" he asked.

I answered that I had been sent to Germany.

"Did you see German soldiers?"

I told him I had.

"They march like this." Forster imitated the goose step with his fingers.

"Goose step," John said proudly. The girls seemed bored.

"They say Germany is pretty. I never see those places again."

After dinner we talked about the chapter meeting and then inevitably about Sally.

"I give her electric coffeepot and some enamel coffee cups. I give her about one hundred fifty dollars' worth of merchandise. I wonder if she give them back. I don't know. It is personal."

JULY 11

AT BREAKFAST THIS MORNING the radio was blaring as usual the early morning program in Navaho which Forster never misses. A race riot was mentioned.

"Why white man bring Negro to United States?" Forster asked.

I answered that it was for labor.

"Why didn't they send them back? It was white man's fault." He laughed and swatted a fly.

He sits at the end of the kitchen table with a swatter at his side at every meal and almost never misses a fly. When he cannot reach it, he hands the swatter to John or me. John seldom misses, but I usually do, and everybody laughs. Once a day Forster pours scalding water on the floor to kill the red ants with which he is in endless battle, and every few days he attempts to flood them off the terrace with the hose. One day, half in jest, he poured hot coffee on the cement floor to kill them.

I mentioned a girl's puberty ceremony I had heard about in another section of the reservation. Forster's only comment was, "Girls have to run plenty at that time." Only Cora has had a puberty ceremony.

"I wake up real early this morning," Forster said, changing the subject. "Four thirty. Even radio station was not on. I dream about Sally. I think she was here."

I asked him if that was why he woke up, and he answered that it wasn't. Then I asked him to tell me more about the dream, but he said it was "just a dream."

Despite the condition of his car Forster drove all the way to Round Point this morning to attend court. He is bored and having a hard time keeping busy.

"There were lots of people," he explained. "Mostly drunks. Drunken drivers. Driving without license. A lot of five-dollar fines. Paul Harper spoke and judge presided. A lot of prisoners were from Squaw Dance."

He agreed to take me to court at the next session.

Forster needs money for his car and mentioned this as we were waiting for lunch. I told him that I hadn't paid him any rent yet, but he ignored this and continued talking about the car.

"Maybe I drive to Carteret in Bill Thomas' car. He say I can use it. Too long to go in this car. All right to go to town, not to Carteret. I have down payment there. Twenty dollars. I bring transmission back."

I asked him who would install it.

"Maybe somebody in town. How much you think is right to pay for rent?"

I told him I didn't know, and he started to talk about Sally.

"She run around too much. She live in big house with other girls but she run around anyway. They drink too much. Not good for her off-reservation. Too much drinking."

"Some people, I heard about," I said finally, "pay five dollars a week."

"Sally she make so little money. Only forty dollars a week. It's not enough. I earn ninety dollars. She even graduate from high school. Forty dollars not much. Some girls they come back. . . . Five dollars a week and buy their own food. That is OK."

I asked him if that was enough. He said it was, and I told him that I would cash a check at the trader's this afternoon.

"Maybe Sally she come back like in dream," Forster
continued, laughing. "I not see her month now. If Hopi
take over factory, she have to quit."

He is ambivalent about the factory. On the one hand he
does not want it to fall into Hopi hands and on the other
he does, because Sally, he claims, would then have to quit
and come back to him. I do not think he is able to admit
his ambivalence.

In the early afternoon a truck dropped off a woman and
two children and drove on. The woman, Forster's second
cousin on his mother's side, was the one who had occupied my hogan the first night. She had stopped by to ask
him to drive her to her camp fifty miles away in return for
a sheep. He was sorry he couldn't accept and seemed worried about her. He went to town and found somebody
who was driving in her direction.

Kenneth Becenti was lying on a cot listening to the
radio and thumbing through *Thorndike's Collegiate Dic-
tionary* when I entered his green clapboard hogan this afternoon. Without getting up, he nodded, and I sat down
on an old writing board which was lying in the middle of
the room near some fence wire. Unlike most of the hogans
I've been in, his is cluttered with odd pieces of furniture
and wooden crates filled with kitchen utensils. Above his
bed he has tacked several big-bosomed, pink-skinned pin-
ups and a newspaper photograph of the Beatles.

Kenneth, a thin boy of seventeen with dull eyes, was
wearing only faded blue jeans. I had already stopped at
his hogan several times but had always found him asleep.
He seemed bored and did not mind talking. He told me
that he and his older brother Tim are living alone this
summer. Their mother is at a sheep camp in the mountains, and their father and brother are farm hands in

Utah, where, as Mormons, they can find work more easily. Kenneth and Tim have both been looking for summer jobs. Kenneth will probably go to Four Corners next week to work as a busboy. Tim is helping his "grandfather" (his mother's mother's brother), who turned out to be Old Man Big Bead, build a fence and will join his father and brother as soon as he is through.

I was surprised at how much trouble Kenneth had in remembering the name of his clan and his father's clan; he knew almost nothing about his parents. He himself was born in School House and went to school there until he left for a vocational high school in Utah two years ago. He has no idea what he'll do when he graduates.

"I don't know much about Squaw Dances," he said when I asked him about them. "I went to one last year. There was a lot of people there. The girls ask the men to dance, and then the men have to pay the girls. I didn't dance. If a man doesn't want to dance, he can say no. They dance for an hour or so, but they sing all night."

I asked him if he had ever had a sing.

"When I was little I was sick and had a sing. It last three days. About four years ago I had another for one day only. I still need two more. Maybe one next winter."

Kenneth was not sure of the names of the ceremonies. He thought the first one was *wolachiji* (Red Ant Way), which he translated as Ghost Way. He remembers only that there had been a hand trembler—"a man who learns things by putting corn pollen on his hands and shaking them"—and that he felt much better afterward. Although he had been in the hospital for a week before the sing, he is "pretty sure" that he would not have recovered without it. He does not recall what was wrong with him. His second sing took place in School House. "There was a medicine man and lot of people around." He himself does not want to become a singer, but he thinks that his father, who hangs around a lot of medicine men, will become one.

When I returned to Forster's I asked him about medicine men, and he explained that in order to become one you have to pay a singer to teach you. Although he seemed interested, he denied any *real* interest. Gene had told me that Forster once started to study to be one but gave it up. I asked him if a white man had ever questioned him about Navaho medicine.

"No," he answered. "A medicine man's business is not their business."

He continues to dissociate himself from traditional Navaho culture in my presence. He seems ashamed of any association with it. Do I inspire this? He seems to be forcing himself to behave in a way which he believes will merit my respect.

At dinner Forster told the children that he had eaten too much "chili" at lunch and had sweated too much. He then poured an excessive amount of cayenne pepper on his stew, and as it got hotter and hotter, he laughed and laughed.

As I was reading in my hogan tonight John suddenly burst in. "Forster wants you," he said, and we rushed out. Forster, who was peering up at the sky, pointed to "moving star." It was a satellite, probably Telstar, moving rapidly across the sky. Everyone was looking at it excitedly. Forster, and even John, bombarded me with questions about the satellite and then about the stars in general. Who make satellite? How big is satellite? Will China get to moon first? Do stars move? Does sun move? What keeps satellites going? Are stars really made of gas? What is gas? Do they burn? I could hardly keep up with their questions. Finally Forster began to talk about the end of the world, and we all listened.

"When end of world come, then all the stars fall down. Book of Revelations says that the moon would turn red and the sun would turn red and the stars would fall down and all the world would be dark."

JULY 12

TODAY WAS PAYDAY. Even before I awoke at six o'clock Harold Kennedy was here, ready to go with Forster and the kids to Carteret to get the transmission. Forster had decided to risk driving the Ford all the way. I was glad I didn't have to go.

At breakfast Forster told me all the things he planned to buy: a new kitchen table and chairs at the discount center, a wood-burning stove which was cheaper than a gas one, and plenty of food. I wasn't at all sure where all the money was going to come from.

On the way to School House we picked up old Deborah King, Sally's grandmother. Forster and Deborah talked and laughed the whole way, and when she finally got out, Forster remarked that he "liked women like that." This contrasts sharply with his reaction to the old deaf and blind woman who stopped by a few days ago. He seemed completely at a loss in her presence. "I can't speak to woman like that," he had said. His children giggled at her and finally gave her a piece of cold watermelon. The old woman lives by herself in a dirt hogan and somehow manages to keep alive. Forster told me that she had plenty of money because she receives a check from the government once a month—the day her relatives come to visit her and share it with her.

As soon as he was paid, Forster set out for Carteret. I spent the morning with Gene driving through the reservation and the afternoon playing with some children and visiting Steven Foster. The children, two boys and a girl, were all under three. Together we improvised toys out of sticks, old tin cans, and rocks. Such improvisation seemed quite new to them.

Steven Foster interested me the moment I met him. He was listening intently, but off to the side, as I collected a genealogy from his stepbrother and then he introduced himself, making sure I had spelled his name correctly and had accurately established his kinship with the other members of his family. He lives at his mother's and step-father's camp near Harold Kennedy.

Steven is a thin, nervous man of fifty-five who has never married. There is something very queer about him which I am not able to pinpoint. At times he acts like a baby or a clown and at others like a suspicious old man. One minute he is trusting and curious, the next mistrustful— almost paranoid—and uninterested.

After carefully establishing my identity and purpose, Steven seemed interested in talking to me about religion and said that he was a member of the Assembly of God and had taken peyote several times as well. He told me where there were peyote churches and then gossiped about the Assembly of God. He saw no reason why he couldn't be a member of both churches. He had gone to Catholic school and sometimes goes to Mass as well because he likes the local priest who, he claimed in an almost dramatic change of tone, is a doctor and wants to operate on him. He said nothing more.

Much to my surprise Forster was already back when I returned. He had bought the transmission but did not have it installed because they wanted too much for labor —sixty dollars.

"Car run perfectly," he said. "I can't understand it. Sixty, seventy miles."

He was going to have the transmission installed in Round Point.

While Forster was picking up Lana and John, a Navaho Tribe truck drove up with three college students who were working as surveyors for the summer. They had come to lay out an acre of land for Forster's house which he had decided to register with the Tribe. The three boys were the most acculturated Navahos I had met; they were proud and haughty and took great pains to talk college slang. One of the boys was studying civil engineering; the second, architecture; and the third, biology. He was especially interested in pathology and thought that he might study medicine if the army didn't get him first. Only the engineering student was sure he would return to the reservation once he had his degree.

Forster returned with Lana, John, and Harold Kennedy. Both men had been drinking and rushed me through dinner alone and then drank together. I was sorry they felt too embarrassed to drink in front of me. Later Forster, Harold, and the kids went for a ride, singing in loud voices.

JULY 13

FORSTER SPENT THE DAY at the garage.

I'm starting to see how kinship operates. The favor is the important thing. Financial dealings are for strangers. Friends are the problem. Forster's friend Harold Kennedy is married to Forster's half sister. Is it this relationship or is it friendship that determines their behavior toward each other? I think it is friendship, though I'm probably making the whole thing too simple. It's so easy to be mechanical. This is my chief problem, especially in trying to understand Forster.

The Navaho don't talk much, and even for a Navaho Forster is quiet. His monotone makes him a master of understatement. Most white men, Gene tells me, think he's stupid and most Navahos consider him intelligent. I just don't know. As far as I can make out, there are two aspects to his life: a substratum of traditional Navaho ways lying below a gloss of stereotyped modern ways. He has never been able to reconcile them—perhaps he hasn't even tried to—and they constantly work at cross purposes.

JULY 14

I SPENT THE DAY IN Round Point checking my population and genealogical data against those of the census office.

JULY 15

GENE DROVE ME to Carteret today. It was good to get off the reservation. I definitely needed a break. I've been feeling emotionally exhausted these last few days. I thought that working at the census office would be enough of a break, but it wasn't.

Forster and his family had also gone to Carteret and returned shortly after I did. The girls had bought some clothes, and John had returned with a new pair of black jeans, a maroon pullover with a white border, and a large bottle of Jade East after-shave lotion. Forster had purchased a hot plate, for which he had been flagrantly overcharged, and a plastic figure of a reclining nude whose removable breasts were salt and pepper shakers. The kids all giggled at this, especially when Forster asked me if I'd seen his new girl friend. They had stopped at the laundromat, and the clothesline was now heavy with wash. The woodpile had also been restocked.

Forster was in a talkative mood and asked me about Gene. He then told me that Lana had stopped by to tell him that she had a date and wouldn't be back until late.

"I tell her I be here on Monday to take her to work. I don't know. These girls they run around. Lana runs around too much. She doesn't tell me anything. Rita tells me always. I don't even know if Lana has a boy friend. They go to Carteret. I don't know. I tell her not to get in trouble. She say, she old enough to take care of herself." Forster laughed. "I tell her I don't want her in juvenile court. I am known here. I know everyone in police station and Judge too. She say not to worry. She take care of herself."

It seemed to me that in fact he had not told Lana any of this and was very upset. He then announced that he had another girl friend, also named Sally, who wanted to go to Carteret with him for the weekend but that he would probably visit his sister instead and come back on Sunday night.

A few minutes later Forster again recounted his experiences at Guadalcanal. He has trouble remembering the name of the island. This time he gestured more freely and emphatically than usual; there was more variation to his voice, which often sounded cruel; and he laughed wickedly, almost hysterically, when he told me about his friend who knocked out the Japanese gold teeth. He seemed far more involved in his story and described the burial scene in even greater detail.

"There was so many Japanese. We line them up in front of ditch and then we shoot. Thirty Japanese each day. I was sergeant. Lieutenant he say, 'OK, Sarge, let them have it.' Everybody shoot." Forster laughed nervously. "And then bulldozer come and bury them."

It was Forster who was in charge of the firing squad and was responsible for the burial. This must have affected him very deeply. He is probably more traditionalist than the Navaho policemen who refused to pick up the corpses at the scene of the accident I had heard about the day of my arrival. The Navaho are haunted by the fear of death. The whole purpose of the Squaw Dance is to kill the ghost of the enemy who is haunting the warrior. Why didn't Forster have one after the war like so many other Navahos? He certainly could have afforded it.

After dinner I asked Forster whether he had any opportunity to make love while he was in the army.

"I had two Hawaiian wives," he answered. "They were pretty, prettier than the Spanish. The Japanese were also as pretty as the Spanish. I never have Japanese wife. There were no villages in Okinawa."

He would have continued, but a red Chevrolet pulled up in front of the house. The white man who was driving —he clearly knew the Navaho—remained in the car for a few minutes and then slowly walked up to Forster, who, rather nervously, beckoned him aside. The two men crouched down under one of the trees and joked for a few minutes and then—I could not help overhearing—the white man asked Forster for the July payment on a loan he had with his company. Forster explained that he had had unexpected expenses—the transmission, his vacation —and would not have the money for another two weeks. The bill collector accepted this without complaint. Forster must have been a good risk. "He's just a friend, a neighbor from Carteret," Forster explained after he had left.

A second car drove up—a black Cadillac. A tall, thin rusty-haired boy with a military crew cut got out and asked us where Lana was. He had gone to school with her and had stopped by to say hello. He had just finished Air Force basic training and was on his way to Vietnam. The boy seemed very disappointed when Forster explained that Lana was not home and suggested he look for her in town.

"That most expensive car in world?" Forster asked after he left. "How much it cost?"

I told him that it cost over five thousand dollars.

Forster listened in disbelief and then said, "My car expensive too. Not many people have one on reservation. It cost me nine hundred dollars and not new."

Later I surprised Forster and John drinking a bottle of California Chianti in the kitchen. They only had time to hide their glasses under the table. The girls, who were watching from their bedroom, could not restrain a giggle.

"That's a good wine," I said, picking up the bottle and looking at the label.

"Yes, good wine," Forster answered, looking at John. "Maybe you have glass. Get him glass."

John poured me an eight-ounce glassful, and everyone —the girls had even come out of their room—watched as I sipped the wine. After I had drunk about half, Forster finally took his glass out from under the table and started to drink.

Dan Shepard, Sally's father, came in, and Forster offered him a glass, which John filled with a vengeance. I noticed that both Forster and Dan chug-a-lugged their wine; John also downed his in a single gulp but consistently poured less for himself. A second bottle was opened.

"This good wine," John said, pouring a glass of the cheaper reinforced California muscatel for the girls who shared it. "Twenty per cent alcohol. The other twelve per cent only." He looked at me disapprovingly. Clearly I did not know wines.

"Twenty per cent, good wine," Forster echoed. "Other good wine too. It cost more. One dollar seventy-nine cents. This one only ninety-eight cents."

"This one better," John insisted. It was the first time I had ever heard him contradict his father—at least in English. "Less money, more alcohol."

"Other taste better," Forster answered. "Dan here you should visit"—Forster turned to me. His face was red, and his voice was already slurred. "He speak good English. Better English than me. Kids speak English but they never talk. Speak English, Dan!"

Dan looked at me with watery, bloodshot eyes and said something in Navaho.

"You see," Forster, who obviously had not been listening, said. "He good baseball player. He was rooky in 1941."

Dan smiled proudly and said, "Forster also good baseball player . . ."

"He hit big home run in 1941," Forster interrupted. "We win game."

"Forster faster runner. Fastest runner. He run like . . ."

Both men interrupted each other as the one heaped praise on the other. The girls giggled, and John poured more and more wine. He was obviously trying to get the two older men drunk. By the time the second bottle was consumed, in less than ten minutes, Dan was asleep at the kitchen table, and Forster was wobbling around on the terrace.

"Key!" John said to him dictatorially. "Car key!"

Without realizing what he was doing, Forster handed him the key. John and the girls quickly jumped into the car—it all seemed planned to me—and sped off, almost crashing into the black Cadillac, which had just turned into the drive. Lana's friend, who had not been able to find her, had returned to see if she had come back.

"He bad boy," Forster slurred. "Bad kids. They drive and no license. Maybe accident. Come, we go get him, find Lana too. Come, let's go," he repeated belligerently to the boy. "You have big car—Cadillac car—we find them. I tell you where to go."

We all climbed in the car and drove toward town.

"I have expensive car too. Costs nine hundred . . ." Forster murmured sleepily and dozed off.

There was no waking him. We returned and lugged him to his bed. Dan was still asleep in the kitchen. Lana's friend left, greatly disappointed, and John and the girls came back safely several hours later.

JULY 16

FORSTER, HIS CHILDREN, and two boys I don't know left early this morning for Forster's sister's. Forster apologized for not having room for me and assured me he would be back early because the girls wanted to go to the local rodeo dance.

Since Forster left his room open to air it and suggested I listen to his radio, I was able to take a good look at the room. Not only was there a complete set of pale veneered bedroom furniture—the only complete set I have seen in Little Bluff—but also several odd bureaus, cabinets, and mirrors. One mirror was almost completely covered with photos: Forster in a sergeant's uniform; Forster, his third wife, and the children; Forster in sunglasses standing next to his car; Sally, a lock of whose black hair was bleached blond; and several unidentifiable ones. Above one of the bureaus a .30-30 and a shotgun were hanging and above another a washed-out painting of Christ. A sheepskin served as a bedside rug. The radio, whose bakelite cover was cracked, and a pile of girlie magazines were on one bedside table; the other held a gray steel paper tray in which Forster had neatly filed away his papers. These included a number of personal letters and letters concerning the organization of his yearly Easter party, at which gifts and secondhand clothes from a Colorado charity are distributed, and also his business papers. Forster pays $456 a year for automobile insurance without personal liability! He has a twenty-four-month loan from one of the best known finance companies in the country for $990.60. His monthly payments are $54, which amounts to a little over fifteen per cent interest per year. He must also pay $305.34 for a two-year-term insurance to cover the loan and interest. His take-home pay is about $80 a week.

Steven Foster was lying on a mattress near a bed, on which four children were dozing, in his mother's cabin. He seemed pleased to see me and greeted me with some warmth.

"I'm pretty tired," he said as I sat down on the floor next to him. "It's a hot day, and I've been working hard —weeding. I've been weeding all morning."

We talked easily about the drought and the condition of the crops, but as soon as I took out my notebook to check a few items from my last interview, he grew suspicious.

"Why you ask so many questions?" he asked.

I tried to explain.

"I've been talking to my lawyer today at the trading post. He came in from Carteret to see me. I tell him about you, and he told me not to answer any questions."

I listened in disbelief and asked him to tell me more about his lawyer.

"I know him because I used to work at the trading post. He's an old friend."

"Is he a white man?" I asked. Steven ignored this.

I explained my purpose in greater detail and put away my notebook. The two of us sat silently for about a half hour. It was midafternoon, and the sun was at its hottest.

Steven's stepfather, Tom Ford, one of the oldest men in Little Bluff, who, like so many old Navahos, received his name from schoolteachers who couldn't pronounce their pupils' Navaho names, came in and curled up on a sheepskin in the corner of the cabin. Steven dozed off, and when he awoke I asked him if he was going to the rodeo dance.

"I never go to dances," he answered.

"Have you heard about the Squaw Dance over at Springs?" I asked.

"I heard them talk about it," he answered, "but I'm not planning on going." He mumbled something about *yeibechai* but would not repeat it. He was probably referring to the large winter ceremony known as Night Way or the *yeibechai* dance which involves the masked impersonation of spirits (*yei*).

Steven said that he didn't know about any local dances and agreed that it was pretty late for the Squaw Dances to begin. He claims not to know the Little Bluff area very well and to spend most of his time up in the mountains with a flock of fifteen sheep. He does not get lonely.

"I'm going to the rodeo," he said, changing the subject. "I'm going to hitchhike. It's about sixty miles from here. I'm leaving pretty soon. I go to all the rodeos. Last year I went to them all and I'm planning to do the same this year. I ride the bulls. Last year I won three spurs."

He grinned.

"I never go to the movies," he continued. "I don't need to. I'm a movie star. I've been in three movies. Once they dress me up. They give me buckskins and feathers. Long feathers all the way down to here." He pointed to the small of his back. "Then they tell us to run across river with tomahawks in our hands and make plenty of noise. The pay was pretty good. I receive one hundred dollars just for that. There are suppose to be some more movies this year. I'm thinking about being in them."

I was reading on the bent garden chair when Forster returned from his sister's without the sheep he said he would bring back. He was drunk and quite belligerent. First he praised one of the boys, who had driven the car back for him, and then ordered the girls to prepare dinner. They accepted his bad mood without complaint.

"What you do today?" he asked in a slurred voice from the car. He had not bothered to get out of his Ford.

I told him that I had visited Steven Foster.

"Did you see Harold Kennedy there?"

"No," I answered. "He left early this morning."

"That's impossible," Forster contradicted drunkenly— and then, "What you learn?"

I answered as briefly as possible, mentioning the rodeo.

"I don't believe it. He never go to rodeo. Just talk. Big talker. That is all he is. He never win spurs."

I asked Forster why Steven never married.

"His thing don't work. It always been that way," he replied.

I wanted to know whether there was anything that could be done about it.

"No, it just don't work. It always been that way."

"Can a medicine man help?" I pursued.

"No," Forster answered hostilely. "I ask *you*, can *you* do anything about it? Do you know?"

I told him that I couldn't do anything about it, though certain white men, psychiatrists, said they could, and I wondered whether the medicine men could.

"That's not what I ask. I ask *you*, can *you* do anything about it?" Forster repeated. He was nearly shouting. It was the first time I ever heard him raise his voice.

"I told you. I can't do anything about it. I thought a singer might."

"No, medicine man can't help," Forster answered more calmly.

I wanted to know whether many Navahos had this problem. I remembered that Kluckhohn had written that impotence was virtually unknown among the Navaho.

"I don't know," he replied. "Those are personal things. I didn't know about Foster until you told me. Do *you* know? I ask *you*, do *you* know?"

I told him that I didn't know any cures. His tone was both belligerent and plaintive.

"These are personal things," he continued. "Do *you* know what a personal thing is?"

"Yes, I know. It is something that concerns—" I pointed to my chest.

"Yes, that's right. That's personal thing." Forster pounded his own chest.

I explained that I thought that he might know because some people talk more than others about their personal lives.

"Who talk more than others?" he yelled.

"Some people talk. They talk about their problems," I answered. "It makes them feel better."

"I ask you who? Who talks more than others?"

"I can give you the name if you want." I felt myself getting angry. "But it will not mean anything to you. He is not from here. He is from New York."

"Give me name!" Forster shouted.

"You don't know him. He's not from around here."

"I know him. Tell me name."

"His name is Pete. Pete Phelps," I said, inventing a name.

"Yes. I know Pete Phelps. He is real son-of-bitch. He is

dead now. I say that he is dead now. Do you understand? He real son-of-bitch. Navaho don't like him. He come out here, here to reservation one time. He is movie actor."

"No, he works for the government," I contradicted. It was clear that Pete Phelps had become a symbol for Forster probably of me and of all white men.

"Yes, that's right. He real son-of-bitch," Forster continued. "We know him out here. He do no good to Navaho. He dead now. Do *you* understand. He dead now. Dead. Do you have any more questions?"

Forster was flushed and out of breath. I decided to ask him again how many times he was married. Although everyone in Little Bluff I have asked has assured me that Forster has been married four times, he has consistently denied this.

"I tell you before," he answered, very hostile. "You even write it down. I tell you I have three wives. Why you ask? Am I right?"

I told him he was right, but he ignored my answer.

"Am I right?"

"Yes, you are right," I repeated. "I was wrong. I asked you. I forgot."

One of Lana's friends, Betty, had come out of the kitchen and was listening to us. Forster caught sight of her.

"Come here, Baby," he called.

She ignored him.

"Come here," Forster commanded.

Betty, who was a big girl of about eighteen, walked over, blushing. Forster pulled her to him and tried to goose her. Betty pushed his hands away.

"What do you want?" she asked.

"She pretty girl," Forster said to me. "Lana have pretty friends. I like big girls like her. Come here."

Betty walked hurriedly to the kitchen. Forster clambered out of the car and hobbled off to the latrine.

At dinner he said nothing to me but bossed the kids around. Betty kept her eyes glued to her plate. The "kids" ignored Forster's advances to their friends. At nine o'clock they all left for the dance, and at one, when I finally fell asleep, they were still not back.

JULY 17

SINCE EVERYONE SLEPT LATE this morning, we didn't have any breakfast. Forster wandered around in a pair of navy-blue pajamas printed with red cottages in the snow. I learned that he had slept in the car while his children were at the dance.

"There were a lot of policemen there," he said. "Lots of people drunk. There was big fight. Kids saw Navaho policeman knocked down. I go to court tomorrow, Round Point, see what happened."

He agreed once again to take me and continued to gossip about the dance.

"No Squaw Dance at Springs. It has been canceled. Somebody drown in spring. Maybe they have it in month, maybe they have it in two months if person drowned is relative of people who give Squaw Dance."

He did not know the details of the drowning or who exactly was giving the dance. He did tell me that there would be no special ceremonies for the drowned person.

He brought out a few cushions from his bedroom and arranged them in the shade of a tree and settled down with a pictorial history of World War II. He showed me a picture of Rommel and asked first if the British had killed him and then if he had been Hitler's superior. I answered and then mentioned that Hitler had committed suicide at the end of the war. Forster nodded. I tried to question him about suicide, but his mind wandered back to Hitler and then Sally. I asked him whether he had liked the army.

"No, I didn't like the army," he answered. "Those who liked it got killed."

He leafed through his book, occasionally showing me a picture.

"It rain a lot in Hawaii," he said as he looked at a picture of one of the Pacific islands. "I there twice. The first time for one month and second time for fifteen days at end of war at rest camp. All we do was to eat and swim and drink beer. PX truck got load of beer every day. No duty, just guards. Keep watch around."

I asked him if there were any women around.

"Yes, truckload comes every day."

Forster continued to muse.

"First time I see big fish was in Seattle, Washington. Two big ones follow us. I think they wanted food. Then there was big round fish. They jump all over. . . . I seen flying fish too. . . . Boat trip back from Hawaii took five days. Band was playing when we left. One day they say we couldn't leave camp. Two days we couldn't leave, and then that night they put us in big truck, and we knew we were going home. Gosh, we was happy. Band play and everything."

"They arrest Willy Murphy," Forster announced suddenly, after a pause of about fifteen minutes. "Four sheriffs, they come from Carteret. Kids passed by and saw it."

I was surprised and asked him what had happened.

"You know, that man killed in Flagstaff at Pow-Wow. They think he did it," he said, referring to the murder of

Red Julius, which I had heard about on the radio. "They also take Harold Kennedy's fingerprints."

I asked him if he thought Harold did it.

"I don't know. When Harold drink, he fight a lot."

Forster then suggested that I stop at Willy Murphy's to see if he was back. He was not there.

"Lana and Martha come back late last night," Forster said at lunch. "John, Cora, and me, we come back *all* alone. Maybe *they* weren't alone." Lana glanced conspiratorially at Martha, who stared at her plate and blushed.

"Lana sleeps on table. She come back *so* late," Forster continued. He was referring to the table in the arbor where the girls often rest during the afternoon. He seemed to be both teasing and chastising the girls. They looked down at their plates, embarrassed, and pretended to ignore him.

"Kids earn plenty of money," Forster continued after lunch. "Lana and John each earn sixty dollars a week. Take home forty-nine dollars. More than Sally make."

I wanted to know what they did with the money they earned.

"They use money to buy clothes."

"I thought the Navaho tribe paid for clothes for children in school," I said.

"Only hundred dollars each year," Forster answered. "Not enough."

When I asked him if John and Lana contributed to the household expenses, he nodded. He seemed embarrassed at my question but proud of his children's earnings.

Kenneth Becenti, who was back on his bed daydreaming when I stopped by, had found a job as a handyman and seemed relieved at not having to go to Four Corners.

Wanting to learn how much he really knows about traditional Navaho culture, I asked him about Navaho clans.

"I don't know much about those things," he began, and with some prodding continued. "It goes through your mother's side. You can't marry anybody who is the same clan as you. You can't sleep with them either. I don't know much about my father's clan. Kids don't pay attention to clans any more."

Kenneth told me that he would marry somebody of his father's clan or his own for that matter. "It doesn't matter any more," he said.

I wasn't so sure. I asked him what the old people believed would happen if somebody had sexual relations with a clan relative.

"I don't know. They say something bad happen. Maybe you get sick. Maybe you go crazy."

I learned that both Navaho girls and boys usually make love before they are married and that there is no special virtue in marrying a virgin. I wanted to know when and where Navaho adolescents have their first sexual experience.

"Maybe when you're fifteen. They usually begin at a Squaw Dance or a social dance. They make love in cars or anywhere."

"Do they wear clothes when they make love?" I asked.

"It doesn't matter. In the old days it did. The people wore clothes then."

"Who starts to make love earlier, boys or girls?"

"Maybe girls, maybe boys."

When I asked Kenneth what positions were used, he answered that you could use any position you wanted. I do not think he understood my question. I asked him if he had ever made love.

"One time. Last summer. It was after a Squaw Dance."

"Did you know the girl?"

"Yes. She was at school with me. I never see her again. She lives in New Mexico. Maybe one of these days I go to see her."

"Where did you make love?"

"Behind a hill near the Squaw Dance."

"Were you dressed?"

Kenneth blushed and nodded.

"What position did you use?"

He shrugged.

"I mean, were you on top of her or was she on top of you?"

He looked puzzled.

"Do you think it was the first time she had ever made love?"

"No, she had a boy friend before me."

"How old was she?"

"Maybe sixteen, maybe seventeen. I don't know."

"Did you know her clan?"

"*Tl'ashchi.*"

Kenneth's clan is *Todachini;* his father's clan is *Khi-yan'ani.*

"Do you have a girl friend now?"

"Yes." He looked down and blushed.

"Have you slept with her?"

"No. I'm planning to one of these days."

"Did you see her at the dance?"

He shook his head.

"Did you like the dance?"

"People fight too much. The police were there and arrested some Navaho. There were a lot of people drinking. I think I saw my brother from Utah there. . . . There's supposed to be a Squaw Dance tonight. I'm not going. I've got to work tomorrow."

"Do you think your girl friend will be there?"

He shrugged.

The subject was exhausted. Kenneth lay back and stared at the ceiling. I had no idea how much of what he had told me was true. I changed the subject and asked him to draw me a map of Little Bluff, which, much to my surprise, he readily, almost enthusiastically, agreed to do. The map was very schematic. Only a few of the many hogans in the area were shown; with one or two exceptions they all belonged to members of his clan or a relative's. Only a few fields were sketched in. He did not indicate the boundaries of Little Bluff or any natural features.

We then talked of life in Little Bluff. The Becenti family does not cultivate any land but often helps the Big Bead family with their horses and fields. Like most families in the area I have talked to, they prefer not to shop at the local trading post, where prices are higher. The trader, who is generally not liked by the local inhabitants, has told me that most of his clientele are not from Little Bluff and are often old customers from around his former store, which was in a more isolated area. They still maintain good credit with him.

"Then we were doctors, lawyers, ambulance drivers, letter writers, just about anything you can name," the trader had said nostalgically. "Here it's different. Things are more commercial."

Kenneth then described the farming methods employed, especially the use of tractors, which seemed to interest him. The plowing of fields is done on a cash basis and is monopolized by a man from town and the Big Bead family.

I was surprised to see Forster still in his pajamas when I returned late in the afternoon. Martha and Lana were so tired, Forster said, that they spent the entire afternoon asleep on the wooden table in the arbor.

Dinner was served even earlier than usual—at four instead of the usual five. Forster finally confessed that he had been drinking yesterday and was too tired to go to the Squaw Dance in town. This was his first mention of it.

"People do not dance at the Squaw Dance," he said. "Too many people drink. Girls are afraid to ask them to dance." Part of the Squaw Dance is a sort of Sadie Hawkins dance, in which the girls drag the men out into the dancing area. The men must then pay the girls for each dance. The going rate is ten to twenty-five cents. "They just sing all night. You can't leave after it starts." Forster was not referring to a ritual prohibition, such as that at a peyote meeting, against leaving the dance, but was simply stating that it was hard to get away once you were there.

After dinner Forster and I sat on the terrace and stared at the cars that drove by, occasionally commenting on one thing or another. He mentioned, for example, that Dan Shepard's fifteen-year-old son, who had dinner with us, is always dirty. He never washes his hair.

"There is sing for Harold Kennedy," Forster announced suddenly. "One-night sing only. I don't know name. Way over there." He pointed to the west. "His relatives live there. It is far away."

I asked him why.

"Because of fingerprints. They say it clean him from FBI people." It is the FBI that handles the investigation of any felonies in which the Navaho are involved.

Forster disclaimed any further knowledge of the matter. The murder of Red Julius has had a greater impact on the people of Little Bluff than I ever suspected. I wonder why Forster had not told me about the Squaw Dance and

Harold's sing until now—when it is impossible to attend. He knows I'm interested in going.

"Dogs sleep all afternoon," Forster remarked after a long pause. "I throw big pail of water on them." He laughed. "They run away. Real far. Don't come back until now."

In the distance I could see Forster's two dogs headed back toward the house. They were followed by a third— an emaciated mongrel with German shepherd blood.

We watched them trotting toward us until we were interrupted by John, who told Forster something in Navaho. (John avoids speaking English in front of me whenever possible.) Forster looked up at the steep wall of the bluff. A drunken man was clambering down the bluff following two girls and in turn followed by an old woman who was trying to stop him. Forster's three daughters came out to watch and climbed onto the roof to get a better view. Lana reported what she saw through a pair of old opera glasses to her father, who listened attentively. He knew the family but not their name. John and the dogs climbed up on a ridge to watch. In the distance I could see a few other people watching the drunk totter down and disappear somewhere behind Howard Lightfoot's house. For a few minutes the bluff had come alive.

John returned with the dogs, and Forster began to tease the new mongrel by stamping his right foot and shouting. All three dogs barked, and Forster and the children laughed. The game continued for fifteen or twenty minutes until Forster ordered John to catch a field mouse he had seen run into the toolshed. Everyone gathered around to watch John search for it between boxes and barrels. Unsuccessful, he went to the girls' room and brought back their cat, which showed no interest in the hunt. Everyone laughed. Forster and I joined in and eventually John grabbed the mouse by its tail and chased after his sisters. Later he gave the by-then-mangled creature to Blackie.

Forster remarked afterward that he had once shot an owl which had perched on the electric pole near his house and another time a blackbird which was eating his corn. Several years ago his two guns were stolen, but he has since replaced them with a shotgun and a .30-30. He occasionally goes hunting for deer but hasn't had much luck lately because there are too many hunters who "come from everywhere, even California."

JULY 18

"I DREAM OF SALLY again last night," Forster announced at breakfast.

I asked him what he dreamt.

"I dreamt she was at home, and I was going to see her. Maybe she come home this weekend."

"She probably will," I said. "You keep dreaming about her."

"I don't think she like me any more," Forster continued. "Gosh, two months, and I haven't been down there to see her."

After breakfast Forster and I drove to Round Point. Forster has been going to court to break his boredom. Several days ago he told me that he usually splits his vacation into two two-week periods, one in the summer and the other in winter, but that he had decided to take his entire vacation this summer because there is more work in the winter. He would have gone on a trip had it not been for John and Lana's work.

We arrived at court several minutes early. A number of

Navaho women were milling around the entrance. They had come to bail their relatives out.

"My father is in the clink," one woman, a very acculturated nurse dressed in starched blue jeans, told me rather embarrassedly. "I was here at Round Point when I learned that my father was arrested for drunkenness up at the rodeo. I swore I'd never bail anyone out of jail and, look, now I'm doing it." She seemed much more ashamed than the other women, who stood around impassively waiting for the court to begin.

Forster and I entered the courtroom, which was nearly full—it seats fifty—and took seats in the last row. Hanging over the judge's bench was a picture of the tribal chairman, and on one wall there was an enlarged newspaper photograph, twelve feet by five feet, of the Rations Issue at Fort Sumner in 1868. Fort Sumner, about one hundred eighty miles southeast of Santa Fe, was the site to which the Navaho were forceably removed after their defeat by Kit Carson in the 1860s. "Fort Sumner was a major calamity to The People," Clyde Kluckhohn and Dorothea Leighton wrote in *The Navaho* in 1946.

. . . its full effects upon their imagination can hardly be conveyed to white readers. Even today it seems impossible for any Navaho of the older generation to talk for more than a few minutes on any subject without speaking of Fort Sumner. Those who were not there themselves heard so many poignant tales from their parents that they speak as if they themselves had experienced all the horror of the "Long Walk," the illness, the hunger, the homesickness, the final return to their desolate land. One can no more understand Navaho attitudes —particularly toward white people—without knowing about Fort Sumner than he can comprehend the Southern attitude without knowing of the Civil War.

I wonder if the Navaho present in the courtroom appreciated the morbid irony of having such a picture in *their* courtroom, modeled upon the court of their conquerors. Later in the day, as I read through a pamphlet prepared by a chief justice of the Navaho Courts and entitled *Know Your Rights in the Courts of the Navaho Tribe,* I felt a similar irony. The introduction, "Chief Justice Speaks," reads:

In our day to day living we are often unmindful of the great influence upon our lives—past influences—persons, places, things, ideas, thoughts, deeds, and actions. As a child is born of its mother we are umbilically tied or influenced by the past. These influences shape our lives and these events may cause us to suddenly veer in new directions.

The work of the Judges of the Courts of the Navaho Tribe is work with the People of America. It is work bound to the past. Indeed, our Judicial Branch was born of the stinging indictment of the past. The work of the Courts is intimately connected with the work of the Creator and Author of all things. This is true, simply because the Court must deal with problems that affect the hearts, hopes, inspirations, asperations [sic] and the life, liberty and property of the human being. The Court must be aware that man is the only thing of importance in the world. The Constitution of the United States affirms this fact. And too, all governments should be keenly aware of this.

The Courts of the Navaho Tribe though only three years of age have been by a few, even well meaning but ill informed persons accused of not developing or evolving more rapidly.

Recent past events vindicate our Court for at least taking a second look at the past. The world beyond the Navajo Reservation is plagued with "Hurry up Justice." And now at this date we are recognizing the deficiencies—the sins committed in the name of Justice.

Our courts are making every effort to become effective gen-
eralists and utilize what other people have learned. We ask
only that our court use the accumulated learning that has rele-
vance to a particular case. To this end we shall not become
bound by meaningless rules.

May the Courts of the Navaho Tribe always pay strict attention to the Wind and the Flame, the "Guardians" of all Justice.

As the twenty-one defendants filed into the room with
guilty schoolboyish expressions on their faces and filled
the first two benches, there was a murmur in the audience. They were all males and ranged in age from boys in
their teens to men in their late sixties. The clerk of the
court, a woman, asked the men if they knew their numbers, and when she saw one eighteen-year-old-boy, Rod
Quinn, who was the son of a Navaho schoolteacher, she
said, "You got into trouble again since you got out of
here. You must have a proud father." After each of the defendants had been told his number again, the clerk noticed me and ordered anyone wearing sunglasses to remove them. I was in fact the only person in the courtroom
with dark glasses on.

Everyone stood as the judge entered and called the
court to order. The first defendant was called to the stand
and questioned in Navaho until the judge caught sight of
me. He stopped short and said in English:

"I want to explain the procedure of the Tribal Court
on the reservation. I want you to understand you are here
only for arraignment. We are going to record your pleas.
If you have committed the offense you should plead guilty
and if you have not committed it, you should plead not
guilty. You will be sentenced at one o'clock today if you
plead guilty. If you plead not guilty, you will have a date
set for your hearing or trial. You are to explain your

home situations and problems which the court will take into consideration if you place yourself at the mercy of the court. . . ."

The first few cases were conducted in English. The younger defendants did not seem to mind; but many of the older ones, who could not understand English, stared at the judge blankly.

Paul D: He is single, unemployed, and eighteen years old. He pleaded guilty to a charge of intoxication in a public place. The judge noted that he had been previously convicted of the same offense and gave him a moral lecture on the seriousness of the charge, especially since he was underage. Paul was immediately sentenced to ten days in jail or a fine of fifteen dollars.

Tom B: He pleaded guilty to a charge of liquor violation (i.e., possession and/or transportation of liquor on the reservation). Tom is an eighteen-year-old, who is unemployed and lives with his parents. The judge asked him if there were any mitigating circumstances, and Tom explained that he wanted to get a job so that he could buy some clothes to wear at school. The judge dismissed the charge in light of these circumstances and the fact that it was Tom's first offense, and asked him to come to his chambers after the court was adjourned.

Rod Quinn: He had been arrested twice during the weekend, the second time while on bail, and was charged with driving without a license, intoxication while driving, reckless driving, offensive conduct, and liquor violation. Rod pleaded guilty to all the charges except the liquor violation and reckless driving. He had had no idea that there was any liquor in the car and couldn't understand how he could be accused of reckless driving when he was picked up in a parked car on a dirt road. The judge explained to him that he would have to have a trial for

the last-named offenses at which he would be permitted to
have counsel but no professional attorney.

"You can obtain advice from the Legal Aid Society,"
the judge explained to the nervous youth, who did not
understand how he was to obtain advice if he was in jail.
"You will be put on bond. This requires two signatures.
The court is unable to appoint counsel because we do not
have any funds for one. We do have funds for the jury,
who are paid ten cents a mile for transportation and a dollar an hour."

The remaining cases were conducted in Navaho. All involved charges of drunkenness. After the court had been
recessed for lunch, Forster disappeared and returned a few
minutes later.

"Judge want to talk to you," he said excitedly and led
me to the judge.

The judge greeted me warmly and said that he was
pleased Mr. Forster had brought me to the court. When
he had seen me, he had decided to conduct some of the
session in English so that I would understand what was
happening. He had evidently heard of me.

"Let me show you the courtroom and my chambers,
which are not much." We looked admiringly at the bench
and the desks. "If you have any questions, I'll try to answer them. There are many things I myself don't know.
Our courts are new—only a few years old. I learn something new every day. I'm always reading and studying—
trying to keep up with everything. It's hard work. I find
these books most helpful." He pointed to a set of *American
Jurisprudence* and a compilation of the laws of Arizona
and another of New Mexico. "We are free to use any American law books, just like any court in the nation, but these are
the best for our purposes."

I asked him what kind of cases the court handled.

"Mostly misdemeanors," he answered. "Most of our cases involve drunkenness. The Navaho drink too much. I understand the situation and try to be lenient, especially with the young fellows. I've only had ten per cent of my cases appealed," he said proudly. "I try to be considerate and take family matters into account. Many young men come in with a charge of drunkenness one time only. I try to give them a chance and have a long talk with them— just like with that boy Tom today. He's been having family problems. You can't blame him for getting drunk. It would be a shame to spoil his record. It's the older ones, who are charged again and again, that I'm hardest on."

I asked him about the jurisdiction of the court.

"Navahos who live on the reservation," he answered. We have all kinds of problems with jurisdiction. We are only ready to handle misdemeanors and cases involving domestic relations. Felonies are handled by federal courts and sometimes by state ones. The court handles only matters concerned with Navahos living on the reservation. We don't even permit our defendants to hire attorneys. They can have counsel—other Navahos who give them advice and aid them at trials. We have received money from the Office of Navaho Economic Opportunity to hire lawyers to help defend members of the Navaho tribe in other courts. This is our biggest problem. Often the people do something illegal without even knowing it and are tried in a court without understanding it. We are trying to stop this."

"What would happen if a white man was caught drinking on the reservation?" I asked.

"We would not have jurisdiction. If you were caught drinking at Mr. Forster's house," the judge said jokingly, "we would have to send you down to Carteret."

The judge introduced me to his secretary and to the

clerk of the court, who seemed relieved to find me on friendly terms with him.

"When I saw you in the courtroom, I didn't know who you were," she explained apologetically. "We don't like to have strangers in our court."

The judge explained that there are six trial judges and a chief justice. The appellate court consisted of two trial judges and the chief justice.

"None of the judges have had any formal legal education. We have all been through training, though, and have attended courts in different states. We sit through court to learn procedure. Our training is very practical. It's just a beginning. We're all trying. Are you coming to the sentencing this afternoon?"

I assured him I would be there, and Forster rushed me off to meet the chief of police, who was less friendly than the judge and told me that it would take a hundred years to learn about the Navaho. He was busy now but would be glad to see me some other time.

"Father of police chief is my uncle," Forster said on our way to Little Bluff for lunch. "His sons call me father." I could find no relation between Forster and the family of the chief of police on the genealogy that Forster had given me. "Judge and me used to hang around together," Forster continued proudly. "We used to go hunting. Once I shoot a twenty-five-quarter deer. I was on furlough just after basic training. I shoot him first thing in morning. Judge was with me."

At lunch Forster told the children what had happened, and afterward we returned to court. I noticed a poster on the bulletin board giving the starting salary of a Navaho policeman at $4160 and the maximum salary of a patrolman at $4940. The policemen are among the wealthiest

Navahos. As I was jotting down these figures Forster came up to me and pointed out a number of landmarks, including three of the four sacred mountains—San Francisco Peak, Mount Taylor, and Mount Hesperis—on a large map of the reservation. He made sure I wrote the names down.

The sentencing started late. More people had come than in the morning, and the defendants, who were no longer guarded by the police, filed in very meekly.

Rod Quinn's case was the first on the docket. He looked as though he had been through hell and impressed me as being somewhat spoiled and conceited. He was clearly intelligent and was obviously prepared to outwit the judge. The judge told him the court procedure and asked him if there were any mitigating circumstances. Rod got up, prepared to make a speech, but suddenly grew shy of the court and explained rather haltingly that he planned to go to college in the fall and wanted to work to earn the necessary money.

"I worked all last year after graduating from high school," he said, "in order to earn money. College is expensive."

The judge agreed, explaining that his own children were in college, and gave him a long lecture on the seriousness of his offense and the difficulty and cost of education. I had the impression that word had gone around among the young people picked up for drinking that the judge was a sucker for education and that he had played right into Rod's hands.

"What are you going to study?" he asked.

"I'm planning on majoring in psychology and philosophy," Rod answered.

"Life can be ruined in a moment," the judge said philosophically. "Drinking can do it. You have a whole life ahead of you and don't want to ruin it. I know how it is about drinking. Life can be difficult, but drinking is no answer. Education is."

The judge dismissed the charge of disorderly conduct, ordered Rod to get a driver's license within thirty days, and put him on sixty days' probation for drinking. The charges of liquor violation and reckless driving would have to be dealt with at a trial yet to be scheduled. Rod evidently realized that he had outwitted himself in pleading not guilty to them and attempted to explain his reasons but in the end refused to change his plea. I wondered how much of the judge's leniency was for my benefit as proof of his liberality.

The judge then recessed the court, explaining in English "for those who do not understand Navaho" that there had been an automobile accident which he had to witness as coroner. There was considerable confusion in the courtroom after this announcement, largely because most of the people had not understood the judge. It was finally agreed to release the defendants to relatives, who would be responsible for their return whenever the session would resume. This was done in a very informal manner.

On the way back to Little Bluff we stopped to do some marketing, and Forster asked me to buy some chewing tobacco and cigarettes for a cousin who was serving a sentence for drunken and disorderly conduct. The judge had agreed to release him two weeks early for good conduct. Forster had spoken to the judge about this before introducing me to him.

Around dinnertime Forster's maternal aunt and her family stopped by and hung around until Forster asked them to eat with us. It is the first time I have seen him hesitate to feed somebody.

After dinner, as we were sitting on the terrace, we saw a four- or five-foot bull snake headed toward the toolshed. Foster and John ran out of the way, very frightened, and much to my surprise insisted that I kill it. After I had crushed it with a pick, they looked at it carefully, and John hid it behind a ridge, where the dogs wouldn't be able to find it. Forster told me that he had once found a snake in his bedroom, which had scared him, and had seen several huge snakes in the Pacific.

Forster invited me to go with him and the children to the movies to see *Our Man Flint*. Second-rate movies are shown at Round Point once or twice a week, and are well attended. At the entrance I met two white friends and introduced them to Forster, who seemed very pleased, especially when they joined us. His own children sat with their friends. The movie was very crowded. Here and there an older couple in traditional costume or modern dress could be seen in the mob of teen-age girls in pastel shorts and boys in jeans and pointed shoes. The auditorium was so noisy that I could barely hear a word of the movie. The Navahos laughed at all of the slapstick but missed most of the verbal jokes and the parody of James Bond, who has yet to come to the reservation. Flint's world seemed so distant from the reservation that I wondered if there were any common points of reference. After the movie, I asked Forster what he thought of it, and he answered that it was good.

"That man, what's his name, sure fights. Japanese fight that way."

I asked him what he thought of the women in the movie.

"Oriental woman looks like some I seen in Okinawa."
The children had nothing to say about the movie.

JULY 19

FORSTER TOOK MUCH LONGER than usual
this morning returning from town, where he had driven
Lana and John to work.

The food has gotten worse because Forster has spent all
his money on the new transmission. Last night we had
chicken which was just beginning to turn—I could taste
it on the meat nearest the bone—because the kids had
waited too long to freeze it.

Forster has been spending most of his vacation sitting
around. At first I thought he would become so bored that
he would begin to talk or offer to help me. But no, he
draws deeper and deeper into himself. He stares at the
highway and the bluff and muses, occasionally dropping a
hint of what is going on in his mind: usually a thought
about Sally or a memory of the army. He keeps telling me
over and over again about the war—a sort of abreaction, I
suppose. It seems to have blocked out his other memories
and has had a strange effect on me. At first I listened out
of curiosity and then I became involved. The last time he
talked to me about Guadalcanal I was nauseated by the
time he was through.

Sometimes I have to remind myself that what may seem
boring to me has significance for Forster. I can describe
Little Bluff or watch a car go by, but Little Bluff or the
car still has very little meaning for me. For Forster they
are filled with meaning that is laden with emotion and is

not only subjective but, more important, shared. He knows whose car it is that goes by, where they are going, what they are doing, whom they are married to, and what their expectations and fears are. None of this is conscious. It is just there. Maybe we are thrown into an alien world, as the existentialists say, but it does not remain alien for long, as we grow into it and it grows into us.

I often forget this as I wander around Little Bluff, trying to understand what is going on and really projecting my own notions onto everything about me. And then suddenly I am reminded. Take, for example, the drunk who wobbled down the side of the bluff a few days ago following the girls and trailed by the old woman. Forster became interested and watched them attentively. The kids even climbed on the roof of the house and reported to their father what they saw through the old opera glasses. I asked who they were and what was happening. Forster said he didn't know, but he did. Not only did he know what the man was wearing but that the two girls were his daughters and the woman his wife. He probably knew where the drunk had bought the wine and what his wife was saying. He was reminded of other incidents—of the drunk who had been seen prowling around the girls' bedroom several months ago, of the hobo who had spent a night in his hogan, of the tramp who had raped and murdered a Navaho girl a few years ago while her brother lay trembling under a bureau with one of his eyes gouged out, of the fury that he and every other Navaho felt when the man was declared criminally insane and disappeared from sight into one of the government institutions far away to be forgotten—and never forgotten. Memories linger here far longer than they do in our world, constantly bombarded as it is by new information. And then maybe Forster will turn and look across to Harold Kennedy's house to see whether Harold has returned from a sing, a purification ceremony he is undergoing because the FBI took his fingerprints—evidently they suspected him of murdering Red Julius at the Pow-Wow arranged by the white people for their commercial interests. He may then turn to me, the white man, who knows nothing about it, and say, "Harold Kennedy not back." I will look at him with a bored expression and wonder why he is interested in Harold's return and how he can tell from such a distance that Harold is not back. I can hardly see his hogan. And then maybe at the end of the day, Forster will explain that Harold has gone to a sing. And I will be surprised and peeved because I wasn't told and wasn't asked, and I will realize how much of a stranger I am and will know that even my learned reconstruction of Forster's train of thought is probably all wrong.

Forster returned from town at nine o'clock. He looked his car over carefully and discovered that one of his tires was losing air.

"They say Harold Kennedy kill man at Pow-Wow," Forster said as we were changing the tire. "He has been gone week now."

"I thought he was at a sing," I remarked.

"Yes, that's what they say, but he disappeared. They found some blood on his shirt, same as dead man's. His wife gone, too."

"I didn't see any police over at his place," I said.

"No, but he gone for long time now. Nobody know where."

"Do you think he did it?" I asked.

"I don't know. He was drunk."

I learned that Forster had heard about this from a medicine man in town this morning. He told him that Harold had been seen with Willy Murphy on the night of the Pow-Wow and then had gone off by himself. When he returned, Willy had seen blood on his shirt, got scared, and left him. Forster seemed worried.

"What you think happen to him?" he asked. "How many years he could get?"

I tried to answer.

"Maybe you go see Dan Shepard or Steven Foster. Anyone. Find out what happen," he suggested and added regretfully, "Yesterday I seen Harold's relative at market and didn't ask. It's lucky he have no kids. If we seen him, even if he was drunk, we would bring him back, day we went for kids?"

I agreed that we would have.

"I tell him not to go to Pow-Wow. I tell him Pow-Wow dirty. He says to me that he go up to mountains near Utah where north wind blow, that I'm right. Then, that morning, he second to hitchhike to Pow-Wow. Only Tall Singer go first."

I told Forster that I would try to find out more and walked over to Willy Murphy's cabin.

Willy was stretched out on his bunk reading a magazine.

"I guess I haven't seen you since the Fourth of July," he began straight away, forgetting that I had in fact seen him since.

"Well, it's a long time. I suppose you heard what happened."

"Oh, well, the FBI has been here a couple of times asking me questions. They been asking me about the one who, well, the one who. . . ." Willy hesitated.

"You mean the one who died in Flagstaff?" I asked.

"No, he didn't die. He was killed. Well, you see, I got my check from the government cashed down there at that camp, what do you call it, that camp just this side of Flagstaff, the one with the trailers."

I told him the name of the trading post where he had had his check cashed.

"Well, I got my money down there. It was the day after the Fourth. That's how they got my name. They're checking, well, they're asking questions of everyone in the neighborhood. They been up here a couple of times asking me questions."

I asked him if he knew anything about it.

"No, that's what I tell them," Willy answered. "Well, they saw that we used to hang around together."

"Did you?"

"Yeah. But I didn't see him that day. And so they come up here and ask me questions. They just keep asking me. They didn't seem to believe my word. 'Why don't you take my fingerprints?' I tell them. 'I'm willing to have a lie detector test, I hope you'll believe me and then leave me alone. It's tiresome. You ask and ask and ask.' All those questions. When I got back that day, they come up and ask. It's tiresome. I came back on Wednesday. I stayed the night before at that camp on the other side of the sawmill. . . .

"I seen that fellow, the one they call Harold, Harold Kennedy, that day," he continued. "He ask me to buy him a hat. Every time I see him, he ask me. Finally on that day, Tuesday, the day I get my check, I buy him a hat. Then he disappeared. That was the last I saw of him. Later they tell me that the FBI picked him up and took his fingerprints or give him a lie detector test or something. That's all I know."

Willy repeated his story several times but added nothing new. I tried to change the subject but he would inevitably twist his answer back to the murder. I did learn that he had been wounded with shrapnel during the war and had been hospitalized for eleven months.

"I get a check for that," he explained. "It comes from the army, from Chicago, on the first of the month. I get another from San Francisco. It's for old age. It comes on the third of the month.

"How do you like my wild Indian?" Willy asked me toward the end of the interview and pointed to a rubberized plaster Indian in a loincloth with a tomahawk in one hand and a scalp in the other. It was the first time he had changed the subject himself and was a sign that he had finished answering my questions. He always finds a way to end our meetings.

I asked him where he got it.

"In Flagstaff." He laughed.

I looked at him, puzzled.

"I thought you meant the scalp," he explained.

On the way out, he asked me if I had any reading material.

"I'm a reading man myself," he said. "I'm reading American history today. All about the American Revolution and Fort Ticonderoga." Willy's magazine was one that dealt with popular history.

I told him I might be able to find something.

I then hiked over to Harold Kennedy's camp, but no one was there. Steven Foster was not around either, but a rather heavy Navaho man with a Mexican look about him was seated cross-legged in the middle of the yard surrounded by children, and was taking old automobile generators apart. He explained that he had spent the entire morning—it was now two—removing the copper wire, which he sells for sixty-two cents a pound in Carteret. He already had three pounds. I asked him where Harold was.

"He's at a sing," he answered. "A one-night sing. They sing and pray over him. It's down there to the west. That's where his family is. On Friday the sheriff was here looking for him. Maybe he found him. Maybe he didn't. I don't know. They say he killed that man at Pow-Wow. I don't think he did it. He gets drunk but I don't think he'd kill the man. . . .

"I learn to do this in Los Angeles," he continued, referring to the dismantling of the generators. "I was there for six months without a job. One day a Mexican comes over and asks me to go with him to a junkyard. They had some generators there. We took them apart, just like this, and sold them. Then we bought some copper tubing and sold it and made a big profit.

"I lived there in L.A. for eleven years. Around with the Mexicans. I worked for a fruit company and loaded and packed cans. I learned English and Spanish. Spanish is just like an Indian language. Maybe a little bit faster. It's easier to learn than English."

The children began to call me names. One little boy called me a sheepdog, and everybody laughed.

"I'm planning on going up to Utah in August," he continued, slapping the little boy jokingly, "to work on a farm. I'll be doing the picking. The Mormons will give me a job. I'm an L.D.S. What church do you go to?"

I told him that I didn't go to church.

"I thought maybe you went to the church down at ———." He mentioned a bar just over the border of the reservation and laughed. "Your friend Forster Bennett likes that kind of church. One day he drinks and the next he goes to church.

"I probably stay up there a month. Last year I was there for eight weeks and earned seven hundred dollars.

That's plenty of money. I didn't have to work for the rest
of the year." He grinned.

On the way back to Forster's, I met Steven Foster. He
playfully hid his head behind a floppy blue hat as I approached him and smiled schoolboyishly when I pretended not to recognize him. He had just come back from
the rodeo and knew nothing about Harold Kennedy. He
hadn't been too successful at the rodeo. He didn't have
enough money to enter.

Forster dropped me off at Gene's when he went to pick
up John and Lana. On the way he told me that he had
moved down to Little Bluff because his second wife had
some property there.

Forster's boss, who was visiting Gene, told me that he
had heard from Bill Thomas, whom I had met my first
night at Little Bluff, that Forster was very jealous of his
brother, the lay missionary, who had been a tank commander during World War II. Forster had only been a
grave registrar, Bill maintained. Forster and Bill have not
gotten along too well because Forster had refused to help
Bill when he first came to work. Bill had complained, and
since then the two men have vied for their boss's favor.

When I mentioned my having to kill the bull snake,
Gene pointed out that this was in line with the traditional
Navaho attitude toward snakes: they avoided them. The
older Navahos would remain in a hogan with a rattle-
snake rather than remove or kill it.

JULY 20

"HAROLD KENNEDY BACK," Forster announced at breakfast. He had seen him last night. "He was at sing. FBI come ask him questions three times. They do test on blood on shirt. It was his blood from bloody nose he got—not from dead man but somebody else."

After breakfast I asked Forster to tell me more about his Easter party, which he has organized for the past few years in different parts of the reservation. He is very proud of the party, which is one of the high points in the year for him. Forster receives old clothes, food, and other gifts from a Colorado Christian charity and distributes them every year at a large gathering of Navahos—a few Hopis and Paiutes have also attended. The Navahos bring food and prepare a meal of mutton, fried bread, and coffee. There is much singing, praying, and merrymaking. Forster showed me some pictures he had taken and his letters of thanks to the charity. I had only time to jot down a few excerpts.

"Many of our people," he writes in one, "did not know what Christianity really was but now many throughout the reservation have turned to the Savior so now they have tasted and realized what it was. Even some medicine men have turned to Christianity."

"There were prayers and testimonies," he notes in another, "and one hundred people came forward to profess the faith of Christ. It is always a thrilling sight to see one, two, many accepting Christ as their Savior because all our

days we the Navaho Indians have been living in fear, superstition, sin and pagan darkness. Now the light of the
glorious gospel of the Lord Jesus Christ is shining in
many of our souls. Many of our people have received and
accepted the grace of God therefore they have peace in
their hearts which were once darkened and fearful and
sinful."

"We thought this was the best location for our annual
party," he explains in a third, "because these people were
neglected from the Christian aspect. Our main concern
was to bring the Gospel to these Christian foresaken Navahos in an isolated area. It is evidently and positively
clear that we reached more people with the intent to ob-
solve these people from their superstitutious
bondage. . . ."

After I had read them and praised Forster for his good
work, he asked me if I would help him draft a new letter
for the forthcoming party.

I decided to visit Colin Curtis today. Although he was
very cooperative when I first saw him on June 30, I have
not gone back to see him, probably because he lives out of
the way. Colin and his five girls were eating under an
arbor when I arrived. He seemed happy to see me, asked
me to join him, and wanted to know whether I had collected many names. After we had corrected his genealogy,
I asked him to draw me a map of Little Bluff and was
startled by it. Although he lives on the northern boundary of the area, as I have geographically defined it, he used
his campsite as the southern boundary and drew a number of camps several miles away in the plains, with which
I was not familiar but which were around his mother's
camp. Only after he had completed this did I ask him to
draw the rest of Little Bluff. This he did in far less detail.

I wonder to what extent kin ties determine area boundaries.

"I'm a Baptist," Colin answered when I asked him what his religion was. "I have nothing to do with peyote. I see church is better than peyote. Navaho religion doesn't help me. I don't believe in it. They take too much expenses for medicine.

"There are some medicine men," he explained in his staccato voice, which is very difficult to follow, "who make sings and others who use herbs and grass. Sometimes they buy them in Carteret. Tom Ford used to be a medicine man but now he's too old. My father, Kitom Curtis, collects herbs and all kinds of woods. Most people today are interested in peyote and not in medicine men. The peyote church meets on Saturday and Sunday, so they have time to cool off. Larry," Colin continued, referring to the man who had helped Forster with his transmission and told me that he had never taken peyote and didn't approve of it, "took it once but he didn't like the way they did it. It went on all night, and he was sick and couldn't leave. Jack Austin used to take peyote for fifteen years and was head of the peyote church and then one day he think it no good for him and went to Baptist church. He says you was harmed a lot."

I asked Colin if he knew a lot about herbs.

"I don't. Kitom Curtis does. One day I follow my father when he collects grasses and bushes. They have a name for all the different grasses. I don't know them."

I wanted to know when people go to a medicine man.

"Somebody have bad dream and they dream they are going to die and so next day they pay medicine man to pray for them. What do white doctors do when you have a bad dream?"

I told him a little about psychoanalysis. Colin seemed

interested but could not understand why telling your problems would help to bring about a cure.

"That's the way peyote work," he observed. "You join the peyote church and then you feel better."

"What do the old Navahos say makes someone go crazy?" I asked.

"If people of the same clan marry," he answered, "the ancestors [the traditional Navaho] say that when they get old the man would go crazy and will have to go into fire and burn himself. Some people have little burns on arm because of that."

"Are there other ways of going crazy?" I pursued.

Colin asked for a pencil and drew on a newspaper he had been reading a genealogical chart to illustrate father's sister–father's son incest.

"Some people do this," he explained, "and they go crazy. Alcohol can make people go crazy. Alcohol makes the whole body shake. Some people drink too much, and they can't drive or eat any more. Their eyes become real round. One time my brother see things. 'The son is coming. The man is coming. I can see them,' he said. The other men said, 'You are crazy.' They wanted to call the police so that they would take him away so that he would cool off. He said, 'There is nothing wrong. I see them coming. . . .' His mother came and put medicine in his mouth and bit his hand to make it bleed a little. He didn't want the medicine. 'There is nothing wrong,' he said. 'There is nothing wrong with me.' Finally they call the police, who come around in a panel truck. He says to them, 'There is nothing wrong with me. The man was coming. I can see.' It may be in his imagination.

"Once when I come home on furlough," Colin continued (he had been in Korea from 1952 to 1954), "my sister told me about a dream somebody had during the night.

She tried to sleep and then she wake up and dream about two bears that talk Navaho and hold each other's arms like this." He crossed his arms over his chest. "She has to walk with bears, and they go into shadows, and bears tell her that visions [spirits] might come up, and they destroy the people by all kinds of weapons like tornadoes. Bear said that then all the people will be destroyed by something like a tornado, unless Navaho keep up with ways of medicine man. Otherwise they will be destroyed by the tornado. Then she woke up."

The bear, I later discovered in reading Reichard, is an important figure in Navaho mythology and a major power in the ceremonial known as Mountain Chant. Although Changing Woman, one of the most sympathetic figures in the Navaho pantheon, gave Bear to the People for protection in their travels, the Navaho, Reichard maintains, have "what amounts almost to phobia about bears, and consider them as primarily evil."

"Some people go into spells," Colin went on, referring to the hand shakers. "They put corn pollen on their arms and they shake and sing. They try to find out what causes patient's problem. They say the devil or ghost has caused it. They say dead man is reason for it. One man tells me that he doesn't remember what he did when he had spells. These stories I heard from dozen people. Somehow it starts happening that way. I don't know what causes it. Some people say that alcohol causes it, and some other people that alcohol is good because doctors use it.

"Some people drink and get drunk and get run over," Colin said, shifting the subject. "Some people say that they get drunk and walk around. If I get drunk, I just fall over and get a headache. Another man takes more and more and more and never has a headache."

He told me that his wife sees a lot of drunks around the

restaurant where she works and then gave me his wife's schedule. He baby-sits whenever he can and pays a neighbor to do it when he is at work.

"Do you believe in flying saucers?" he asked me.

I told him that I didn't but couldn't be sure.

"I don't know either," he agreed. "I've never seen one. It may just be in the imagination.

"This is a story I hear from my father when I was little," he said after a short pause. "Maybe a million years ago, they had no sun. Then the earth was kinda small. They started to make the sun in a hogan. They make the sun day by day. The men have to make up mind who is to carry it. One man [the one who was to carry the sun] divorced his wife. When the wife was with him, he made her sick. When the man goes over the hill [goes away], she feels better. Another man comes to the lady, but the first man looks back over the hill and finally sees the man coming around. That man makes love with her. When the first man comes back, the woman tells him she is sick. 'How do you know you are sick?' the man asks. 'I know,' she says. 'If you are sick, why did that man sleep with you?' he asks. That meant that the man had seen her. He was not jealous. He just left. He did not beat her. It [adultery] is the same problem today. It is the same problem year after year. People are just like that today. Then the first man has to carry the sun. If he had been jealous, he would have had to drop the sun. He carried the sun every day, and then he came back to the hogan. 'Why are you back?' the people asked. 'I forgot one thing,' he says. 'When I carry the sun, what do you give me for it? I have to decide myself what you give me for it. From now on when I carry the sun, some of you will have to die every day.'

"That is what the old people say," Colin commented.

"But I don't believe it. If nobody dies, then the sun might stop." He laughed.

"I learned a lot of stories from my father but I forgot most of them. Compared with Bible stories, I don't believe them. Do you want to hear another?

"A woman tried many medicines but finally she died. After fourteen days the people went to her grave. In those days they have only graves and not cemeteries like today. And they found that the grave was empty. The lady went out somewhere. They went to the canyon. 'Maybe she is there,' they say. They look down at the edge, and there is the woman below, combing her hair. From that day everyone will go below when they die. She didn't say anything. She just looked up at them. You go into the earth when you are dead."

Colin asked me to tell him the white man's stories about the sun, and I told him about Apollo and Prometheus.

"There are all kinds of signs in the Bible about the coming of the end of the world," he said after I had finished. I do not think that he expected to hear Greek myths from me but, rather, Biblical tales. "My father says that pretty close to the end of the world there will be a sign. Then the dogs' noses will drop off. Then we are close to the end of the world."

He then told me that he knew parts of a lot of stories but not the whole thing. He explained that Coyote started alcohol. "He collected woods and juices so that people would drink every year." As I was leaving, he promised to remember more stories to tell me when I came back. I felt very relieved. At last I had found someone, even if he spoke poor English, who was willing to tell me some of the Navaho tales. In fact, I would have preferred to learn the tales from a man who was not a traditional Navaho

but who had had fairly intimate contact with white society. It would be interesting to look for thematic differences between the traditional and the contemporary versions.

"That man Colin is the only Christian in that family," Forster
said later, after I had told him where I had been. "What you
talk about?"

"He told me a lot of interesting Navaho stories," I answered.

"Well, he was a bootlegger," Forster remarked. "He had
been a bootlegger with his brothers for many years. I bet
he didn't tell you that."

I shook my head.

"Now you see," he said. "You never know."

Forster had done nothing all day but move a few stones
which served as a border for his trees. He had dozed off
and had almost fallen from his garden chair. He told me
that he was going to take down the fence which surrounds
his property—his camp is one of the few fenced in in Little Bluff—and put it up again along the lines marked by
the student surveyors. He will put up some wagon wheels
to mark the entrance to his property.

"One day Howard Lightfoot come over," Forster said
proudly. "He asks me where I got wheel. He wanted
twenty. I tell him I got them from dead man's wagon."
Forster laughed. He and the accountant seem to compete
with each other over their houses.

JULY 21

FORSTER WAS ALREADY AT WORK on the fence before five this morning. He was very proud of this and told me that he had seen Willy Murphy and Tall Singer hitching into Carteret when he got up.

"Today we go to Grand Canyon, see Rita," he said at breakfast. He had mentioned a trip to the canyon several times before and had invited me to come as soon as he learned I had never seen it. No date had been set for the trip.

I asked Forster what time he planned to leave.

"Nine o'clock. Rita does not get out of work until three. We bring her back then. You have plenty time to see canyon."

I returned to my hogan to type notes, and at eight I looked out the door to see if anything was going on. Forster and the two girls, Cora and Martha, were waiting patiently for me.

"I'm ready whenever you are," Forster called.

We loaded a gallon jug of water in the car and piled in. The girls were quiet throughout the trip. I tried making conversation but as usual failed.

As we approached the canyon, Forster asked me whether we had scenery like that in New York and then what it was like in Germany. I told him that there were a lot of little towns in Germany, each with an inn, where you could get good beer, and a church.

"A church!" Forster interrupted. "Germans not Christians."

I told him they were Christians and that it was Hitler

who had advocated a return to the earlier religion. I
started to tell him about German mythology, hoping to
stimulate conversation, but he showed no interest. I had
no choice but to lose myself in the scenery, which was
spectacular. The mountains and the pine forests stood in
marvelous contrast to the dry reservation.

We drove on to Grand Canyon Village and waited
around the restaurant where Rita works, wandered
through the curio shop, and watched the tourists. I
pointed out a German to Forster, who looked in utter fascination and laughed when the German bowed to the people he had been talking to in a slightly exaggerated fashion. I wondered what Forster imagined them to be like.
He was far less interested in a French couple who walked
by. After we had waited for a half hour, Forster finally left
a message with a Navaho girl, who works in the restaurant
with Rita.

"There is good cafeteria over there where you can eat,"
Forster pointed out, and he seemed pleased when I told
him I preferred to buy some food for everyone for a
picnic. After we had bought some bread, cheese, and sa-
lami in the village market—Forster remarked that the
prices were less than in town—we drove to the picnic
area. Forster and the girls got out of the car and immediately began to look for piñon nuts as I prepared the sandwiches and opened the cans of soda. This impressed me as
a sort of withdrawal, because there were in fact no piñon
nuts around. They were all very embarrassed but ate
heartily when I offered them the sandwiches and soda.

After lunch we drove to the canyon rim. Forster told
me that he had once decided to walk across the canyon
but hadn't had time yet to do so, and then asked me if
there were any dinosaurs around when the canyon was
first formed. I answered that there probably were but that

there were no people then. He was startled at this.

Forster and the children settled down on a bench over-looking the canyon to wait the three hours for Rita, and I wandered off along the rim. I got caught in a rainstorm, and when I returned to the car, Forster and the girls, who had all been asleep, laughed at my bedraggled condition.

Rita appeared promptly at three, and they all went off to a "living room" to talk. Forty minutes later they returned, having decided not to bring Rita back with them, as they had planned, because she had to work the follow-ing afternoon. The entire trip—a whole day—had been spent in learning what could have been communicated in a word over the telephone or by letter. Forster and the girls did not seem to mind.

On our way back, we stopped at the market to stock up on food and wine. Forster asked me to drive and had a long drink of California rosé, which he bought for the oc-casion. He grew more talkative and told me about his first day in the army.

"We was sent down to Albuquerque for the physical. Somebody on bus have bottle of whiskey, and I guess I drink a little too much. I could get up all right but soon as I get off bus I sit right down on ground. MP comes up and takes me to jail. At four o'clock they come around with one egg—no, there were two eggs, and some old cof-fee that tasted terrible. Real old. And they had some oat-meal, which was mostly water. That's what they gave us. And then colonel comes in and says, 'Where are my boys?' He calls names and my name was called. I go with him." Forster laughed.

"For two days we wait around for physical examination. At night we stay in big tall hotel. Way high up. There was telephone by the bed. We call up and tell them to bring up some whiskey. Elevator boy comes up with glasses and ice and whiskey and we drink all night. . . ."

I asked Forster about his missionary brother.

"He was a tank destroyer," he answered with little emotion. "He blows tanks up with anti-tank weapons. He was staff sergeant. I almost catch up with even though he was smarter. Just one more stripe. My name was put up for it. I didn't want to volunteer.

"One time I was bust," he continued, "just after I finish Basic. I was Pfc again, real soon. I was corporal by the time we was in Seattle and sergeant in Guadal— How do you call it? Yes, that's right. I was sergeant there.

"I don't talk back much, but one time, I was in Texas, I was working with my head down. Sergeant come up and says, 'Hey, Bennett, what you think you're doing, herding sheep?' And I say, 'This is sheep country, sergeant, ain't it?' Sergeant was real mad. Later when I finish Basic I tell sergeant that I see him in Japan but I never did see him there."

I asked him when he was busted.

"That was in Pennsylvania," he answered. "I go to dance and met a girl. Later I tell her I have to go, and she tell me, 'No, don't go back, come home to bed with me.'" Forster attempted to imitate her voice. "I go and then I fall asleep. Then it was morning. I say I have to go. She says, 'Come on, Baby, just one more time. I need you.'" He laughed. "What could I do? She was pretty. Blond hair and all. So I stay and was late.

"I used to receive two letters a week from my wife," he continued after a long pause. "She was good woman. That's why she die. All good people die. Just like President Kennedy. She even have sing for me when I was away."

He remained quiet for a long time and then told me about a hunting trip he had when he was on a furlough.

"There was three of us. We went hunting just this side of Carteret. We shoot four in one day and give one to white man. It was real early, and I was sitting in front of a little canyon smoking. There right in front of me was a deer. I shot it, and then another come out and begin to run and jump. I shot it. Just under ear. The other man also shoot two. The third one was just like white man; he had no luck. Four deer too many. Only allowed three. White man—he come from California—sees us and comes over. We say, 'Mister, you want a deer?' He says, 'Sure.' He was from California four days and didn't get anything. It was his last day. He takes deer and comes back with bottle of whiskey. 'You boys thirsty?' he says. We said we were but didn't ask him for anything.

"Then there was elk I seen one day. Next day I come back with friend. He says to me, 'You must be crazy. There ain't no elk there.' 'There is. I seen it yesterday,' I tell him. Then the elk comes out of the bushes and I shot the son-of-bitch. It was sure a big son-of-bitch. Big horns, too. We cut it up and loaded it on the back of a pickup. White man he sees us and says, 'You damn lucky son-of-bitch, you Indians.' We bring it back to reservation. I sell horns and skin. We have big feast with plenty of steaks. It was good but a little tough, too old. But you take what you can get."

The girls were fast asleep in the back of the car. They almost never pay attention to what their father says. The effect of the wine was beginning to show on Forster, and I was exhausted. It was a great strain driving Forster's car down the winding mountain roads. It had no emergency brake. After dinner I went to bed early. Forster and the children stayed up drinking.

JULY 22

FORSTER AND HIS FAMILY slept late this morning. When I awoke, I found the girls asleep on the flagstone terrace in front of the house. On the way to town Forster mentioned Kitom Begay, who had evidently gotten so drunk last night that he passed out. John, who was going on a school trip, looked very sleepy in the back of the car. He had brought along a bottle of Mennen's medicated after-shave lotion.

I hitched a ride to Round Point to see the Navaho police chief to ask about the murder of Red Julius. He was non committal. He was not handling the case and knew only that the murderer had not yet been found and that Red Julius had probably died from a blow on the head with some sort of hard object. When I mentioned the concern about the affair in Little Bluff, especially since several of the inhabitants had been questioned, he said that he had heard about it but couldn't understand why there had been a sing for Harold.

"There's a big difference between the old and the new Navaho," he explained. "I asked my father about it, and he said he thought there should be a sing. I told him that I didn't think so. Just questioning. It wasn't a murder charge. He wasn't in jail."

We then talked about juvenile delinquency on the reservation. Although it is now rare, the police chief wouldn't be surprised at an increase.

"A lot of it is brought in by the white children who live on the reservation," he remarked. "They learned it somewhere else and bring it here when they move on the reservation with their parents. I don't think there is too much JD among the Navaho kids living off-reservation. There's a big difference between the Navaho and white criminals. The Navaho are more docile."

The police chief changed the subject and told me about an old Navaho war code which is now forgotten. I asked if there were any fights between the Navaho and the Hopi.

"There aren't too many problems between the Navaho and the Hopi," he answered. "Sometimes there's a fight. Usually it's over land problems. You know that we're fighting the Hopi in the Supreme Court. It's been going on for years. I suppose they'll settle someday. Land is our big problem. . . ."

Before excusing himself, the chief gave me a few copies of the Navaho Police Reports to look through. I spent several hours poring through them. The most outstanding offense was disorderly conduct, which made up, for example in 1964, about fifty per cent of the charges.

JULY 23

TODAY I ATTENDED a Nieman kachina dance on the Hopi Reservation. It is the last dance of the cycle. The kachina bid farewell as they leave for the spirit realm. A number of Navahos had come to see it.

JULY 24

GENE, WHO HAD GONE TO THE RODEO, remarked on how much it had changed since he had last seen it two or three years ago. It seemed more like a hang-out for teen-agers now.

JULY 25

FORSTER HAD GONE TO THE RODEO and was sick. He had diarrhea—"I eat too much boiled mutton and melon"—and a charley horse from fixing the fence. Looking very green, he asked me to drive John and Lana to work. I gave him some medicine for the diarrhea.

When I returned, Forster seemed a little better. He showed me an award he had received for working for the school for twenty years.

"Principal one day he say, 'Tomorrow there is picnic. Come and bring kids. There will be hamburgers, meat loaf, and ice cream. Be sure to come,' he say. Then we go. There were lots of people. Everybody ready to eat when principal get up and call my name. He give me award and fifty-dollar check. I didn't even know. There were four of us. Some white men and one other Navaho. I get fifty-dol-lar check. Twenty years.

"I got letter from Colorado," Forster said a few minutes later. "They're going to deliver some packages to Frank-lin. Lots of work. At Easter party they bring lots of clothes, in big boxes. Each box has label: children's clothes, baby clothes, men's clothes, women's clothes. They also bring lot of milk. There were ninety-seven kids, and each kid got five cans of milk. Extra milk was taken to hospital for Indian babies when they sick and then go home. Mothers can take it. That night they also left some clothes at school for kids. Blankets too. Good blankets. Two dollars each. They still use them at school."

Forster remained silent for a few minutes. It was clear that he wanted to say something but could not quite bring himself to say it. Finally he told me that he would like to visit his sister but didn't feel up to the trip and had no money for gasoline. I told him not to worry. I would drive him and lend him the money for gasoline. He could put it against my rent. He seemed relieved. I drove to the garage for the gasoline and then picked him up. He told me how to go and then settled back in thought. After we had driven a half hour, he suddenly informed me that there was a medicine man at his sister's place and smiled.

I asked him if there was a sing.

"Yes, five-day sing. It is at my sister Emma's hogan [the daughter of Forster's father by his second wife]."

"Who is the patient?"

"A relative," Forster answered. "I give you his name. Jimmy Redway. You write it down." He was referring to Emma's son-in-law.

"What is the name of the sing?"

"I don't know in English."

"Tell me in Navaho."

"*Na'atoe ba'aji.*"

Later I checked this and found it to be the ceremonial known as Shooting Way, Female Branch. This chant is used to cure the prenatal effects of an eclipse and, more commonly, diseases caused by lightning, such as colds, fevers, rheumatism, paralysis, and abdominal pains.

We turned off the main highway and drove across a windy plateau to a camp consisting of two hogans and a brush arbor. A few older men, who were sitting under the arbor, greeted Forster and informed us that two white students had been attending the sing since the first day. Forster suggested I take a look at the sand painting.

The hogan where the ceremonial was being held was

dimly lit. On the western side, opposite the entrance—all hogan entrances face east—the singer, or medicine man, who turned out to be the brother of Forster's friend at the BIA, Dermot Lewis, knelt and gave instructions to four older men who were making a sand painting. The medicine man would occasionally refer back to a cloth pattern in his medicine kit, a battered suitcase. For the most part, though, both he and the painters, who were not singers but merely older, more experienced relatives of the patient, knew exactly what they were doing as they let the black, brown, white, and yellow sands flow from between their thumbs and index fingers in intricate designs onto the paddle-smoothed sand base. To the left of the singer sat a handsome middle-aged woman, whose complexion had an almost copper sheen to it. She was silently braiding necklaces and wristlets of fir boughs and corn husks. Near the entrance the two white students sat, haggard and tired. They had had very little sleep since the sing began four days ago. Occasionally one or another of the men who sat under the arbor would come in to see what progress had been made or to add a few coals to some smoking embers at the hogan entrance. One of the students explained to me that the patient would inhale the fumes of the coals during the sing proper.

I watched the painting for an hour and three quarters, until noon, when the woman had completed the necklaces and wristlets and given them to the singer. I was impressed not only by the dexterity of the painters but by the relaxed atmosphere in the hogan. There was talking and laughter. One of the students was even asked to help with the painting.

When I finally left the hogan to stretch my legs, Forster, who was sitting under the arbor, called me over to join him and then without any prompting, and much to my surprise, began questioning several of the men about their family and clan affiliations. A young man of about twenty, Albert, who turned out to be Kenneth Becenti's brother who had been in Utah, seemed so eager to make a good impression that he would interrupt Forster's translation with his own.

Robert Pyle, the first man Forster questioned, was a tall thin man in his late sixties, who, I learned later from one of the students, is considered to be the local fool. He told Forster that he is not related to anyone here and just goes around helping people when they ask him.

"He says he is ninety-five," Forster translated, "but I don't believe him. His father was Little Mexican, and his mother was Big Round Lady. He has many brothers." Forster listed Robert's brothers. "His oldest brother is medicine man. He is also medicine man. He says he was born in 1918 and is the *Ma'ideshagijni* clan. His father is of Mexican clan. He says that he is big medicine man but is not participating here. He is just visiting. He knows the *naghe'e* sing. This is against white men, Mexicans, and foreigners. It is same sing I have," Forster added, "when I go to army. Tom Long Hair was medicine man."

Naghe'e hojonji, to give its full Navaho name, may be translated as Enemy Monster Blessing Way and belongs to the Blessing Way group of ceremonials, which are the most common and provide good luck, good health, and blessing, especially when the patient is in a somewhat critical situation, such as pregnancy, or has experienced a bad omen, such as having a coyote run or an owl fly in front of him. Blessing Way sings, which may also be used to obviate the bad effects of mistakes made in ceremonials, to dispel fear resulting from bad dreams, to protect flocks and herds, to cure insanity, and to consecrate ceremonial paraphernalia, were frequently sung over Navahos who entered the army.

I was somewhat surprised to hear Forster candidly admit to me that he had been sung over. He added in contradiction to his earlier statements that when he returned from the war he had had a Squaw Dance. I tend to dismiss this. He seemed somewhat carried away—he has a tendency to identify with, or exaggerate his relationship with, whatever is going on about him. A good example of this was his claim that he was related to the chief of police after he had introduced me to him.

"He says he is also hand shaker," Forster continued. "He has no white man's religion because he is a medicine man. He has no sheep, no horses. He says he also knows *hojonji* [Blessing Way, both a generic name and the name of a specific sing] prayers."

"Good Place or Well Fix prayers," Albert translated.

"They sing these prayers the first night of this ceremony," Robert explained. "There was also sweat bath."

"This sing," Albert interrupted, "is just like the Christian Way. It is Navaho religion. Religion of our people."

"Robert Pyle is jealous a lot," Forster continued to translate. "He is not going to tell you his secrets. He receives a check for old age. It is sixty-six dollars each month. He trades at High Point. When he sings, he gets paid. Maybe ten dollars for a sing." Robert Pyle was talking much faster than Forster was able to translate. I had the feeling, however, that the frequent shifting of subject was not just the result of this difficulty but that it was characteristic of him. Several of the men laughed at him. I wondered whether the whole thing wasn't a put-on.

"He doesn't play cards or gamble. He never dances," Forster translated. "He is not woman-crazy. He has been single all his life. He has house and is ready to marry, but he doesn't know who yet." Everyone laughed except the patient, who sat to the side listening solemnly. Robert Pyle seemed quite oblivious of the laughter. "He just waits for right woman. He will never cut his hair because he believes in the Navaho way. If a man cut his hair, his crops will go bad. He learned to be medicine man from his grandfather, Evan Hall. He used to follow his grandfather around, and his grandfather taught him how medicine works. Some people have to pay to become medicine man, but he did not, because Evan Hall was his grandfather. He was told by him to hold these secrets and now he has the true words. He doesn't know this sing today, *na'atoe ba'aji*. You have this sing if lightning comes close to you or if you dream about it. Jimmy Redway was scared by lightning and then he dream about it. That is why he have sing. You dream about it and see it inside your eyes. You will always think about it in your heart. Then you have the sing."

Forster stopped. The men continued to talk about the sing. Albert told me that they said there are two kinds of Shooting Way: a male kind and a female kind. There are also holy ones and "bad" ones. Albert became too interested in the conversation to continue his translation.

"This man is also medicine man," Forster said, pointing to a short, squat man in his middle fifties. Later one of the students told me he knew only parts of several ceremonials. "His name is Big Begay. He says that he is not going to tell white man anything. It is going to be secret for the rest of his life. He dreamed that he landed on moon. He traveled seven days to get from here to moon, and there he saw a relation and shook hands with the relation. He might go back to the moon. He told missionaries and other medicine men about dream, and they just laughed and called him crazy. He will not tell white men his se-

crets, because they will just laugh. He learned his secrets
from old people and nowadays young people, kids, are
going bad. Boys and girls do not even know how to say
hello to their mothers and brothers. They are wild in
their ways. There must be an end to the world soon. His
grandparents told him this. Old people in United States
die, but Navaho will be living on the moon. He saw a lot
of people there that he knew. He heard a rodeo and saw
nice clear water. It took seven days to return. When he
woke up, it was early, five o'clock."

"That is the way it goes," Albert said philosophically,
"just like Christians."

I returned to the hogan. The sand painting was almost
complete. I was told that one *yeibechai* figure had still to
be drawn and that this was a small painting. It was about
five feet in diameter.

"Sometimes paintings bigger than hogan," one of the
painters explained. "Maybe ten, maybe twenty men work
on it."

When I asked if I could make a copy of it, I was told
that this was impossible. I was able to jot down a few de-
scriptive notes. The entire painting, whose geometric figures all represent various mythologically significant char-
acters and objects, was contained within an incomplete
circle—a full circle has harmful connotations for the
Navaho—around which black figures representing a bird,
possibly Black Hawk, were intertwined in an almost ba-
roque fashion. In the center of the painting a second circle about three or four inches in diameter enclosed four
unconnected lines which formed an incomplete square.
The painting was divided into quadrants by what I was
told were *yeibechai* spirits at the cardinal points. I was
given the name of only one of these abstract figures,
Dontso, the Messenger Fly. Between each of these were

representations of the four sacred plants—corn, squash, tobacco, and beans. The entire painting was dominated by a disproportionately large black figure in the east-southeast sector of the circle, near the edge, which jarred with the rest of the painting by breaking up its almost perfect symmetry. This, I was told, was *Djabani,* the Bat, who has thin wings and flies at night. Associated with darkness and of a somewhat ambivalent character, *Djabani* was a personage of the lower world and is in sand paintings one of the eastern guardians.

1:25 P.M. The patient, Jimmy Redway, dressed only in gray shorts, entered the hogan and sat down on a pile of new blankets in the northwestern corner. He was a short, muscularly well-developed man in his late thirties or early forties, whose stomach was beginning to bulge in typical Navaho fashion. Jimmy was anxiety-ridden: his face was taut, his eyes shifty and nervous, his complexion lusterless, and his body tense. Occasionally he would eye me or one of the white students—I wondered if he thought our presence would hamper the efficacy of the ceremonial—but for the most part his eyes remained lowered. (Throughout the ceremonial he maintained a solemn expression and listened attentively to the singer's words. When the medicine man manipulated parts of his body, such as his hands or legs, his response was stiff.)

1:30. The singer, who is stationed on the western side of the hogan, sprinkles pollen—a symbol of spiritual energy used in all ceremonials to drive away evil and to mark out the symbolical path of life—on the sand painting and then walks across it, paying little heed to smudging it as he places four prayer paddles and a number of feather sticks upright on the western rim of the circle. He drapes the necklaces over the paddles. Between the patient and the medicine case the singer places several containers of herbs—a large blue enamel pan and several glass bowls.

1:35. Four men, seated on the southern side of the hogan, begin to shake hide rattles. The singer begins intoning low-pitched, nasal chants, which remind me of work songs. Friends and relatives of the patient enter until the hogan is very crowded. Seventeen people, including six women, three young children, and two adolescent girls, are present. Forster sits on the doorsill, slightly outside the circle of ceremonial activity. The singer rubs the patient with a herbal mixture and prays over him. When the prayer is finished, the patient rubs himself vigorously with more of the mixture.

1:40. The medicine man rubs a turquoise-colored stone on a whetting stone and makes a blue spot, about an inch in diameter, with the powder in the center of the patient's chest between his nipples. A second blue spot is made in the center of the patient's back.

1:43. A man adds more coals to the burning embers at the door of the hogan. Martha and Cora enter with a young boy, whom I have seen around Little Bluff. The singer paints jagged black lines which extend from the blue spot on the patient's chest to his shoulders and then two more black lines across his abdomen in a downward direction. I notice that designs are always started from the center outward; the same procedure was followed in making the sand paintings. Chants begin and end during this part of the ceremonial. Before beginning the third chant, the singer says something which makes everyone laugh. He then paints black lines from the spot on the back and joins them with those which extend from the chest.

1:50. One of the rattlers hands his rattle to one of the students, walks over to the patient, and begins to help the singer with the painting. The white student is encouraged to shake the rattle, and everyone laughs at his efforts. The singer's assistant traces the black lines with white and then blue while the singer draws black lines on the patient's legs.

2:05. Black lines are drawn on the patient's arms. Although the singer continues to chant, the members of the audience begin to gossip. The patient remains solemn.

2:10. A two-and-a-half-year-old boy begins to cry. Everyone looks at him, and he is led gently to his mother, making sure he does not step on the sand painting.

2:13. The assistant traces yellow lines alongside the black, white, and blue ones. The singer gives the patient a herbal brew to drink. After he has finished half of it, he washes his hands in the remainder and then drinks it up.

Albert Becenti nudged me and whispered that he would like to explain to me what is going on. When I asked him to do it later, he insisted that it be done now. I reluctantly left the hogan, and the two of us walked over to a truck where we were hidden from some women who were preparing a meal in front of the second hogan. Albert seemed anxious, and I had the impression that he regarded his conversation with me as a sort of betrayal of the old people. We sat down inside the cab of his father's truck, and he began to tell me almost compulsively about his life, making sure that I wrote everything down. I was annoyed but let him talk.

"I was born in March 1, 1948, and I remember when I was seven I started first grade in boarding school. All my brothers are in school. I graduated from junior high school and then went to Salt Lake City. When I got there I found a job and started to work instead of going to school. When I finished work, I couldn't get back in school because I missed the first semester, and it was already the second. Now I am in the —— Boarding School.

There I passed a full year in three months. Now I have only one more year to go."

Albert must have noticed that I was becoming more and more annoyed, because he changed the subject. "I had a grandfather. He told me about the Navaho Ways. He was a medicine man too. I used to listen to him and watch him." Albert paused.

"Have you ever seen Robert Pyle perform?" I asked.

"No, I don't see him. I stay with father and mother, and there are five of us in the family. I had one sister, and she died I don't know when. I think they tell you about shaking hands. Hand shakers put corn powder on hand— left hand, no, the right hand—and then they shake and they think of something that caused the illness. He says what kind of medicine man is needed. He says he needs a medicine man, a Squaw Dance, a *yeibechai* dance. He needs this. First time they put yellow pollen they say prayers for twenty minutes. My mother used to like it. She still do it but every time she do it she gets sick. Medicine man told her not to be a hand shaker. She gets money, or gifts when people don't have money, when she makes hands shake. Sometimes she gets dollar. Sometimes now she does it. That is first thing."

Albert then told me where the different medicine men he knew lived.

"Next week," he continued, "I'm going to California, just for a vacation. My older brother Tim goes to college there in Oakland."

I asked him what Tim was studying. Kenneth had not known.

"He is studying welding, advanced welding. I don't think I'll be going to college. In two months I'll be heading for my physical. The army will get me before I finish school. Maybe Vietnam."

Albert told me that the Navaho were different from other Indians. When he was in Utah, the Paiutes "raised hell." Then he listed the benefits of education. "I know two languages. That is a good thing." He looked at me for approval. "I took Spanish for three months. It was not too hard. I don't know different Indian languages. I have heard Paiute, Geronimo, Pima, and, oh yes, Hopi." I tried on several occasions to steer the subject to the sing but without success. I did learn that Albert would have a sing before he goes into the army. "It is the only way to live," he said.

Although I would have liked to talk to Albert longer—I was particularly interested in the contrast between him and his brother Kenneth—I was anxious to get back to the ceremony, so I stopped the conversation. Albert seemed slightly hurt.

2:55. The chanting continues. The singer and his assistant have completed painting the patient's body and are now working on his face, which they have colored black across the eyes, turquoise on the nose and upper lip, white on the forehead, and yellow on the lower chin. The medicine man says something that makes everyone laugh; someone asks one of the students for a piece of chewing gum. The student hands the gum to the singer, who begins to chew it and a second piece he has taken from his suitcase. When the gum is soft, he sticks it in the patient's crew-cut hair: one gob ⁄over the left parietal bone, the other over the right. "His hair too short," someone explains.

3:04. The singer walks over the sand painting, which is now badly smudged, puts both necklaces over his shoulder, and sprinkles herbal water on the painting and then on Jimmy. The patient picks up a pair of new doeskin moccasins, into which the singer pours some sand, and then puts them on. The medicine man grasps with his right hand the patient's right arm and holds it for thirty or forty seconds. He then raises the patient, leads him eastward around the smoldering coals and sits him in the center of the painting. He puts more chewing gum in Jimmy's hair, gives him more herbal water to drink, circles him with the prayer paddles, pressing them against the patient's chest at the completion of each circular movement, and does the same with the feathered prayer sticks. The medicine man then removes the necklaces from his own shoulders, swings them around the patient, places one over the patient's left shoulder, the other over his right—pressing, almost hugging, him as he does this —puts a turquoise necklace on the patient, and attaches feathers to the gum in his hair.

3:20. Jimmy Redway seems particularly anxious. The singer's assistant picks up the blue enamel pan, containing still another herbal water, which both the patient and the singer have tasted, and hands it to Forster, who takes a long swig and rubs a little on his face and arms where his muscles ache. He takes a deep breath and looks satisfied. The pan is then passed around to each of the spectators, including the students and me, who all take a long draft. The remainder is finished by the assistant and the rattlers. While the brew is being passed from spectator to spectator, the singer gives Jimmy something else to drink. Forster brings in more coals and places them near the patient's legs. After Jimmy inhales their fumes, the assistant extinguishes them with water, the steam rushing to the patient's face.

3:30. The singer waves the prayer sticks over the patient's head, and as he presses them against the patient's feet and other parts of his body he makes a sound.

3:31. The singer presses a prayer paddle against the patient's head and feet and then places it in the patient's palm and stares at it as he continues to chant. He grasps Jimmy Redway by the ribs, raises him, and sends him out of the hogan. The medicine man destroys the sand painting and places a rug over where it has been. The chanting ends. Jimmy is called back in and seated on the rug. The singer sits opposite him and washes his own hands. He is given Kleenex to dry them.

3:37. A basket filled with gray corn mush is placed in front of the singer, who makes an X on it with yellow pollen.

3:40. The singer gives the patient some of the mush and takes some for himself. After this has been done several times, everyone in the hogan takes some. It tastes sickeningly sweet and mealy. We all file out of the hogan, leaving the singer and the patient alone. Dressed, the patient comes out smiling and quite relaxed, and disappears over a hill to the east. I do not see him again.

Everyone stood around the hogan for a few minutes until one of the rattlers *ordered* the students to clean up the hogan, and everyone laughed as the two tired men carried heavy blanketloads of the sand from the painting several hundred yards to the northwest. The women whom I had seen preparing food in front of the other hogan brought over mutton, fried bread, coffee, and lime Kool-Aid, and I took some to Cora and Martha, who had retreated to Forster's car at the end of the afternoon ceremony. Albert Becenti asked me how I could eat such food, and I told him I liked it. We sat around for about an hour and then Forster announced that we had to leave. I was sorry to miss the final ceremony, which was to last all night, but I had to drive Forster, his two daughters, and their little friend Harry Young back to Little Bluff. Everyone slept the whole way back but Harry and me.

When we returned, Forster immediately set to work on the fence. Later he told me that it was a good sing and that he felt better.

JULY 26

I HAVE BEEN ATTEMPTING to understand the ceremonial by considering its effect on me. During the ceremonial itself I tried to become involved—to empathize—and although I wasn't there for the whole thing and even missed the final night, I got an inkling of its mood and effect: prolonged care and attention, during which time the patient and the other participants become more and more exhausted (and suggestible?)—five days with little sleep—surrender to the authority of the singer, identification with mythological figures which culminates in sitting on and later destroying a beautiful sand paint ing that took hours to make, and the final sharing of herbal waters and ritually treated corn mush with every-one present. This is not to mention the sweat baths, bull roarers, etc., which I did not see, and the constant chant-ing and rattling, which had a dulling, almost hypnotic effect. No trances, though.

Aside from all this I was surprised by the relaxed atmo-sphere of the sing—some gossip and quite a bit of joking. The medicine man was quite a *bricoleur*. Chewing gum! I didn't detect the compulsive quality I expected. It was a very human experience.

Forster had gone, I suppose, to share in the benefits of the sing. His attitude was curious. He was a little like a cosmopolite on a visit to a country cousin. It seemed to me he couldn't quite bring himself to acknowledge his belief in the efficacy of the sing, which I am sure he felt deep within him. Even though he stayed on the periphery of the ceremonial, he was the first to be given the herbal waters and after he had taken a long drink and rubbed some on his aching muscles he took a deep breath and did look satisfied. Was his getting to work on the fence as soon as he returned to Little Bluff a test? I don't know.

There are a couple of children who are beginning to follow me around. I like them and find it relaxing and revealing to play with them. A few days ago, as I was returning to Forster's, the wind began to blow the sand so hard that I had to go into a nearby brush arbor for shelter. Some children were playing while their mother was weaving a rug. I asked them to draw me some pictures and their mother smiled: What a nice young man to keep my children busy. A few minutes later, a little boy came in playing with a fly-infested dead rat and showed it to his mother and me. She smiled just as she had at me.

JULY 27

SINCE THE SING Forster's attitude toward me has changed subtly. He seems much more direct. Today, for example, he asked me straightforwardly for the rest of the month's rent and then to help him drive an old school friend to Carteret tomorrow. There was none of the usual hesitation and circumlocution. I was somewhat taken aback later in the day when he literally burst into my hogan and said, "I go to Frontier [the border town where it is legal to buy alcoholic beverages] with Harold Kennedy and his wife. You come. You drive." I had been watching Harry Young (the little boy we drove back to Little Bluff from the sing, who seems to have moved in with Forster's family) draw pictures, and when I asked Forster to wait five minutes, he snatched the paper from Harry and quickly sketched the map of Little Bluff he had refused to draw for me a few days ago. I suppose he feels privileged now that he has shown me something he knew I wanted to see.

Both men were pressed tightly against each other in the overcrowded car—the kids had come along for the ride as well—and at one point Harold accidentally placed his hand on Forster's thigh. They joked about this and, later, about the nude that was a salt and pepper shaker, which was still in the car.

"We was talking about old experiences when we was young," Forster explained, "when we was running around. I was telling him that I was at the dance on Saturday. I seen so many girls. They was running all over the place. I don't know where the boys were."

Earlier Forster had attributed the evident scarcity of boys to the war in Vietnam. He told me that a boy from town had been sent directly from Germany to Vietnam and wondered whether his son would also be sent. The girls, Cora and Martha, had listened attentively and seemed worried.

"There's going to be a Squaw Dance this weekend," Forster said a few minutes later. He explained that the first night of the ceremonial was going to be in town. "Maybe I go. Maybe not." I couldn't help thinking that he knew damn well he would go and was only saying this to make me realize my dependence on him. I was very irritated because I had been asked to drive so that Forster could drink and still get home safely. I decided to bombard him with unrelated questions which had been puzzling me. What was the name of Harold Kennedy's sing? How many days did it last? What was Forster's first wife's maiden name? Where does she live? Much to my surprise I learned that she lives in Round Point. Forster answered all my questions mechanically and did not seem particularly anxious to talk about her.

At the trading post in Frontier, Harold's wife bought a sack of corn meal, some potatoes, and a few packages of luncheon meat. Forster and Harold disappeared into the bar with the girls, who came back a few minutes later with some soda and Cracker Jacks for Harry and me. When the men returned, flushed with wine, I drove them back in silence. Everyone was asleep except Harry. He is a curious boy—sometimes alert and helpful, sometimes dull and distant.

When we returned, the girls prepared dinner, and Forster offered me a glass of rosé. John, who had returned from work, again complained to his father about the cost of the wine. Forster ignored him and, much to my surprise, began to complain about Gene. "Navaho don't like him any more. He never visits Navaho any more." It was the first time he had ever complained to me about Gene or, for that matter, any other white man. By chance Gene stopped by a few minutes later with a letter for me. Forster offered him some watermelon and enumerated all the things he had shown me. He seemed particularly proud of the trip to Grand Canyon—he mentioned the German tourists —and joked about the two white students who did all the work at the sing. This had evidently made an impression on him because he told the same story to Dan Shepard yesterday.

After Gene left, I went to my hogan. Forster and Dan, who had stopped by, continued to drink. I noticed that two of Harold Kennedy's neighbors also joined them.

But just as I was about to go to bed, Dan burst in. "There's trouble," he shouted. "Some drunks here. We go to police station." I rushed out in time to see two figures slinking off into the dark.

"I get kids," Forster slurred. "Then we go to police. You tell them how that man, what's name, Keith, jump me and try to beat me up."

I didn't know what he was talking about and decided to ignore it. We drove to the station, and as soon as we arrived, the girls jumped out of the car with unexpected determination and ran into the station house—only to stop at the water cooler. The Navaho police sergeant seemed most unsympathetic but promised to send a car over to have a look. He took Forster's name and then Dan's and dismissed them peremptorily. On the road back to Little Bluff, Forster told me that the sergeant had said that they couldn't accuse anyone of being drunk if they themselves had been drinking. Forster was very humiliated.

When we got back he told me that the two drunks were still around and were coming over. I could see two men in the distance. John suggested I go over and talk to them. He called to them, and they came over. They turned out to be Harold's neighbors, who had been drinking with Forster and Dan. I told them that they had better leave because the police were coming. Forster tottered over.

"You listen to him. He knows." He put his arm over the shoulders of one of them and said sadly, "Keith, go home. I went to police. They come any minute." Both men looked at each other mournfully. "Go home, but first shake hands with this man. He from Columbi Un'versty."

JULY 28

EARLY THIS MORNING, as I was typing my notes, Harry came into my hogan. He had spent the night in John's room. Harry is twelve years old and has scruffy black hair, which is usually tinged red with dust. He has an older sister and a younger brother and sister. His father died a few years ago, and his mother has recently remarried. My genealogical records reveal that his younger brother and sister, ages three and one respectively, are probably illegitimate and that his mother is considerably older than her present husband. I have been impressed by her capricious attitude. Since the time I saw her ignore her little boy wailing under a brush arbor, I have watched her carefully dress her little baby daughter in the neatest clothes I've seen in Little Bluff and patiently play with her for hours. Harry seems to move around from family to family in Little Bluff. He is not related to Forster.

I asked him to finish the drawings he had started yesterday. His drawings of a man and a woman, in comparison with those made by the other children on the reservation I have tested, are immature. The man, who is drawn in considerably more detail than the woman, is in traditional dress and smiling. He is wearing a necklace with a large stone, unquestionably phallic in nature, hanging from it. Four "buttons" lead down to the crotch, which is squarely cut off by a belt and low-slung pants. Harry had considerable trouble drawing the hands, which are spiderlike, and in the drawing of the woman they are hidden behind her back. The woman has large eyes and ears, a heavy mop of hair, and little facial expression; no shape is discernible under a sheath dress. When I asked him to draw anything he liked, just as the other Navaho children did he drew a landscape: two brown hogans, black smoke coming from a chimney, brown mountains, and a yellow sun. He included a wagon. Although the somber colors are typical of other drawings I have collected, some of the children his age have used more varied colors. All of Harry's drawings are very lightly—hesitantly—sketched and took considerable time to finish. The first sketch took twenty-three minutes.

When I asked Harry to tell me the happiest thing that had ever happened to him, he turned red and said he didn't know. The same thing occurred when I wanted to know the saddest thing. When I asked him to tell me a story, he grew embarrassed, scraped his feet against the floor, and coughed nervously. After ten minutes, he began very hesitantly.

"A little girl is dead. That is all I know. Last night she died. She eat something. I don't know. I can't guess it."

He stopped. I encouraged him to continue. After a very long pause, I asked him why the little girl was dead.

"I don't know. My grandmother say that."

"When did your grandmother say that?" I asked.

"Two days ago."

"Did it really happen?"

"I don't know. She ate something."

"What makes people die?" I asked. Harry was extremely nervous.

"I don't know. The other is a car. At Pow-Wow somebody got heart attack. That is all I know."

"What happens when they die?"

"I don't know. There is a land over there."

"What is it like?"

"I don't know."

"They killed one cow and two horses in Mines," Harry said, after a long pause.

"When?"

"About five days ago."

"Who did it?"

"A tiger. I mean a lion. A lion killed two horses and one cow. They say lion was big. They say they're going to kill it. My cousin went up there."

Harry then began to talk about bicycles. There were several in my hogan. John had promised him a chain for his bike. He claimed his chain had been stolen yesterday. Twice he told me whom the bicycles in the hogan belonged to.

"Somebody got accident last night," he announced suddenly.

"Where?"

"Down at . . . car, truck, diesel . . . at the market."

I asked him to draw me another picture. He sketched in pencil a very crude landscape and then crayoned over the lines. A heavy black road ran over the mountain. On one side was a hut and on the other a hogan. Near the hogan was a black mass, presumably the underside of an overturned car or truck.

Throughout the conversation Harry was very nervous. He looked down at his feet most of the time and had great difficulty in articulating. There were long pauses between his sentences. He seems unused to conversing. I have, in fact, seldom heard Forster's children or any other children in the area ask questions or initiate conversation. Cora and Martha did not say a word to their father all the way to the Grand Canyon and back, and hardly said a thing to each other. Harry is of course exceptionally laconic. I do not think that he is unintelligent but rather very repressed.

Forster came into the hogan just as Harry had completed his drawing of the accident and asked me if I wanted to go to Window Rock, the Navaho capital. He had arranged to drive Pete Floyd there. Pete is a chapter secretary from a nearby district and is Tall Singer's son-in-law. Forster explained that Pete was related to him because Tall Singer was his, Forster's, uncle. I was sure some sort of financial arrangement had been made between the two men, though no mention of this was made to me. Harry asked to come, but Forster said no. Later he told me that he would like to have taken Harry but could not assume the responsibility.

"I don't know what is wrong with that boy," he said. "He never goes home. Spend all his time here. His mother, she begin to talk. Maybe she says I take away her son."

Cora and Martha did come. They remained silent in the back seat during the entire round trip, which lasted about ten hours. Pete, a rather heavyset man who is much more outgoing than most Navahos I have met, sat between Forster and me and talked the entire way. At the end of the trip Forster commented, "That Pete he sure talk a lot. I can't do it. He never stop talking all the way to Window Rock and all the way back."

I had driven both ways and had taken advantage of Pete's talkativeness to ask him a number of questions on the Navaho religion, and only wish I could have remembered everything he said. The first hour or so was devoted to a detailed summary of Navaho tribal history with particular emphasis on Navaho-Hopi land disputes, which Pete claimed was the reason for his trip to the capital. I had considerable difficulty in getting used to his slurred English and remember little more of the monologue than a barrage of dates. Pete was very careful to give the exact year of each event he narrated; his style reminded me of Forster's recapitulation of his life.

As soon as the occasion arose, I changed the subject to Squaw Dances by asking Pete to explain when they are needed. He answered by example. When he was in school in Oklahoma, he "married a white girl"—she was in fact half Cherokee, half white—and four months later she died in an automobile accident. He felt very bad. He had bad dreams and always felt weak and sick. Finally he went to a hand trembler who told him that the woman's spirit was bothering him. The spirits of the dead, Pete later explained, are jealous of the living and therefore haunt them. A stargazer told him the same thing. As both diviners recommended a Squaw Dance, Pete's family arranged for one, and he felt much better afterward. He did not have a second Squaw Dance after military service, because he had had an accident in San Diego and was hospitalized for six years and had four operations. He would not tell me about the accident or the operations but explained that he had had both Blessing Way and Shooting Way ceremonials at that time. He does not think he would have recovered without them.

Pete then explained that when people die their relatives may talk about them for four days only, and then they must never mention the name of the dead again. When I asked him where the dead go, he became very vague. "They go on living," he said, "but in a different world, which is still around here."

Pete seemed much more anxious to talk about stargazers. They use different kinds of stones, he explained, and look at the stars and can tell things. The light of the star reflects off a topaz, for example, and points to the source of a problem. This is one way of finding something that is lost. Sometimes the reflected light flashes around and around in a big circle. The stargazer is able to interpret this also. You cannot go to a stargazer when you are sick and ask him to find out whether you'll live or die. He can only tell you what is the cause of the illness. He cannot tell you whether a pregnant woman will give birth to a boy or girl. "For that," Pete said jokingly, "you have to ask the moon." There are certain things that a pregnant woman and her husband should not look at "because they will leave a mark on the baby." Pete gave sand paintings, *yeibechai* masks, and the dead as examples.

We stopped at a cafeteria for lunch. Pete and the girls remained in the car while Forster and I bought hamburgers and soda. Forster kept eying the waitress, a rather heavy woman in her early twenties. Later he told me that she was very pretty.

After lunch Pete confided to me that he thought the Hopi "were going down." He had seen many of their ceremonies and has noted their decline. Formerly the Hopi medicine men were able to force snakes out of their holes for the Snake Dance by means of prayers alone. Now they have to use sticks. He has seen Hopi boys take pictures of ceremonies and sell them to white men.

As we passed some ruins, Pete told me that they were the homes of the people who lived here before the Navaho came out of the earth. First Woman had told the Navaho that when they came to the earth they should live between the four holy mountains and the four holy rivers, for here they would dwell in peace for a long time. Pete wondered what happened to the old people who lived here before the Navaho. Perhaps they were destroyed by floods, he speculated, either before the Navaho arrived or while the Navaho took refuge in caves.

Throughout the trip Pete called attention to various landmarks where he had had some untoward experience.

It was here that he was almost hit by a car three years ago. The floodwaters were so deep around this bridge that they had to wade out knee-deep to see if it was still there before passing. . . . They used to spend the night here when they were in school in Oklahoma. . . . Two years ago he bought a goat from the people who live in that hogan. . . . A man hit a horse here and one of the horse's legs landed on top of the car; he saw the car again two days later—the horse's leg was still there; it was frozen on. . . .

Window Rock is clearly an administrative center. The Navahos here all look "officially and politically involved" and are developing the characteristic mannerisms of the *petit fonctionnaire*. I stopped the car in front of a large hexagonal building, a giant hogan, which is the headquarters of the Navaho Tribal Council. Pete went off to find out about his meeting, and Forster left in search of his son Douglas who works as an accountant in one of the tribal offices. He came back a few minutes later with a young man in his early twenties dressed neatly in jeans and a gray cowboy shirt. Forster introduced us, and after shaking hands "in the white man's way," Douglas told me that he had heard about me from his father and then invited us to his house after work to meet his wife. Forster explained, much to my surprise, that we didn't have time. Cora and Martha were both happy to see Douglas, and Forster seemed very proud of him and told me that when he himself was young he was "handsome just like him." After Douglas had returned to work, Forster told me that he was doing well and buying a brand-new Chevrolet sedan. He was going to California for a vacation and had promised to take Cora with him. I glanced at the two girls but could make out no sign of excitement or jealousy. In a rather expansive mood, Forster asked me if I wanted to

meet Robert Arthur and went off in search of him. I wondered what he would tell the tribal chairman, whom he
did not know. He returned a few minutes later alone.

"I didn't get to talk to Robert Arthur. Too many people around. Come, I show him to you."

We walked into the giant hogan. The council was in
session. Arthur's opponent, Don Alexander, was speaking.
The room was large and airy. Some representatives were
busy taking notes; others were sleepily nodding their
heads in agreement or disagreement—I couldn't make out
which. As we backed out of the room we bumped into
Pete Floyd, who had returned to tell us that his meeting
had been canceled. Neither he nor Forster seemed
particularly concerned about a wasted trip involving a full
day and several hundred miles. We drove into Gallup to
do some shopping Food is cheaper here and you can buy
wine and beer.

On the way back we stopped for a picnic. Forster had
bought exactly the same kind of food as I had on the trip
to Grand Canyon. Pete talked all the way but was considerably less coherent. He had consumed nearly a six-pack
of beer. I suspected that much of what he had to say was a
product of his imagination rather than an accurate report
of Navaho lore.

The *yeibechai,* Pete explained, are spirits that man in-
herited from the animals which lived a long time ago and
were as big as dinosaurs, because the animals had wanted
to live forever. All the Navaho songs and prayers had always existed, even before the advent of the Navaho, who
had learned them from the air. The air sang into the ears
of the Navaho just as birds sing. When Pete was young,
his father forced him to run naked in the snow and ice
and sing as he ran. Not only did this make his arms and
legs strong, but it strengthened his lungs so that he could

become a *yeibechai* dancer and singer. This is the hardest kind of singing, because you have to hold the pitch for a long time. *Yeibechai* dancers are not allowed to have sexual intercourse during the sing and for several days afterward. Pete has been paid to dance a lot of these dances. There are either six or twelve dancers. *Yeibechai* dances are held only in the winter and Squaw Dances only in the summer, except in case of an emergency. Other ceremonials can be held at any time, but these two are different because they are both social and religious.

Pete shifted to his favorite subject. Stargazers must kill an eagle. They take the fluid from the eagle's eye and put it in a pouch where it dries up. This enables the stargazer to see as well as an eagle. Just as birds eat worms so eagles eat snakes. For this they need good eyes. Medicine men and witches make pouches from the bladders of bears, eagles, deer, and snakes. The bladders contain a poison which can be used as an "anti-poison." Pete was growing less coherent. He had pulled out a can of beer from a paper sack at his feet and was drinking it in large gulps. He explained that there are Indians in South America who use blow guns with poisonous darts and suggested that witches use similar instruments. Navaho medicine men do not use them. All animals have protection against snakes. He doesn't know exactly what kind of protection bears have, but deer have little sacks under their eyes and on the inner side of their hind legs. When they step on a snake, the liquid in the sacks drips down on the snake and paralyzes it. The deer can crush it with its hooves. Medicine men also make use of these sacks.

As we passed some jimson weed (*Datura stramonium*), Pete explained that it makes you crazy if you eat it but that it can also be used as medicine. Once, when he had a festering wound, his father wrapped jimson leaves over it, and it got better. He pointed to another brush, which I couldn't identify, and told me that when two of the entangled branches accidently graft onto each other, a married couple will stay together for a long time. "This is a superstition," he said, "just like a white man's superstition."

I asked Pete if he went to church. He answered first that he didn't and then that he went to whatever church happened to be closest. They are all the same. In 1930 a new religion began, he explained. It is the peyote religion. Pete doesn't approve of it: the Navaho learned their religion from First Woman, and she said nothing about peyote. It makes you see pictures and you go crazy from it. It's just like locoweed. He learned from a friend that in Mexico they give it to bulls just before a fight to make them angrier. If you look at something for a long time and then take peyote you'll see it under the spell of the peyote. It's used for political purposes. Once he stopped in at a peyote meeting and caught sight of a picture near the leader, who tried to hide it, but Pete saw it. It was a picture of a candidate for councilman. The people who saw it under peyote would never forget it and would have to vote for the candidate.

Pete again pointed out landmarks significant in his life and told several rambling tales about murders and jailbreaks. One of these involved the man who taught him silversmithing. He had been chased all over because he had rustled white man's cattle but was never caught. A second dealt with the murder of a Hopi by a Navaho. The Navaho got away because the sheriff didn't like the Hopi.

We drove by some mules. Forster looked up and groggily told me not to hit them because then we'd have to eat them and "they taste almost as bad as beef."

By this time Pete was very incoherent and began to elaborate a theory of hand-eye coordination which enabled Buffalo Bill to shoot at and hit tin cans thrown into the air and stargazers to point out the cause of a problem.

It was dark when we arrived at Pete's camp. He introduced me to his daughter, a sixteen-year-old who spoke excellent English and looked very pretty in the flickering light of an old lantern. I was very tired and asked Forster to drive the remaining thirty miles home. He had begun to irritate me toward the end of the trip by warning me several times not to hit any stray cattle crossing the road at night. "Maybe you have to pay one hundred dollars," he had said.

JULY 29

AT BREAKFAST I ASKED Forster if he was going to the Squaw Dance. He said he wasn't sure, but if he did he wouldn't stay long. There was too much fighting at Squaw Dances nowadays. I spent the morning typing up what I had learned from Pete Floyd and was interrupted around eleven by Forster, who came to collect the last ten dollars I owed him for the entire summer's rent. The representative from his finance company had stopped by to collect the July payment. After he had gone, Forster finally explained who he was and told me that many Navahos borrow from his company. It advertises extensively on the radio, and I have noted that Forster takes a certain pride in being associated with the company whenever he hears one of its announcements—a pride not unlike that taken by a small stockholder when he passes by one of his company's buildings. After lunch, Forster turned to me and said, "Let's go to dance." I was surprised, for although

I had been sure that he would end up at the dance, I had never expected him to leave so early. The ceremony does not begin until sundown, when the patient delivers the prayer stick to the stick receiver for inspection and safe-keeping.

When we arrived at the stick receiver's camp at one o'clock, preparations for the evening were well under way. A large brush arbor had been constructed for the occasion. Women were preparing mutton, fried bread, coffee, and lime Kool-Aid; men were slaughtering sheep and chopping wood; and children were running around, wide-eyed and excited. The stick receiver was wearing new doeskin moccasins with shiny quarters for buttons, a purple velveteen shirt, pressed Levis, and a red fillet. A large turquoise necklace hung from his neck, and his belt was studded with silver and turquoise. Solemn and aloof, he wandered around and would occasionally give directives. We remained in the car watching. Harold Kennedy, who had come early to help with the preparations, signaled us to come over, but Forster remained in the car.

"I'm afraid of all those women," he said embarrassedly. "They will make me chop wood."

A quarter of an hour later Harold beckoned to us again, and this time we joined him. After Forster had greeted a few friends, he led me into the arbor, where we were served mutton and freshly fried bread by Forster's mother-in-law (the maternal grandmother of the children who are living with him), Hannah Cody. Hannah had clearly made a special effort to find us choice pieces of mutton. Martha and a friend joined us, but Cora remained in the car.

"I don't know what is wrong with that girl," Forster commented. "She is too shy." I have the feeling that despite her curlers Cora, of all his daughters, is the most likely to end up living in a dirt-floored hogan in traditional dress.

After we had finished eating, we walked over to the ceremonial hogan, where the patient or his substitute will present the prayer stick. A few men were lying around sleepily on sheepskin rugs. Occasionally one or another would mumble a few words to no one in particular. Soon everyone dozed off, and when they awoke a half hour or so later, they began conversing in Navaho. Forster ignored me for the most part, though at one time he pointed to a drum and told me it would be used in the ceremony. He then began to tell a story in Navaho which captured everyone's attention. It was Big Begay's dream-trip to the moon, which had made a very marked impression not only on Forster but on all the Navahos who had heard it.

By two fifteen, the hogan was empty. I had started to follow Forster and Harold Kennedy, but for the first time Forster told me that they wanted to be alone. I wandered around by myself. About fifteen cars and trucks had arrived. The women were still busy preparing food, but most of the men had disappeared into the shade over a nearby hill, where they were drinking and gambling. From the distance I spotted Forster and Harold playing cards. Several men in their twenties came up to me to find out who I was. They seemed a little hostile and told me that Squaw Dances were for people who had had contact with white men, Hopi, and Chinese. One of them started to add Apache and then corrected himself.

"They say that being with a foreigner makes you sick and then you have to have a Squaw Dance," he explained. "It's like a pow-wow," a second added. "Everyone meets relatives and friends."

"It's not just social," the first corrected. "If somebody

sees a dead man, they think that they are sick and decide to have a dance."

I was told that the Squaw Dance lasts three days. Tonight the people from the patient's party are the guests of the stick receiver, who is not a relative but a friend. They will sing and dance all night, and in the morning the stick receiver's family will give presents to the patient and his family. They will throw them from the smoke hole in the ceremonial hogan. The second night will be spent midway between the stick receiver's and the patient's camp. Again there will be singing and dancing. On the morning of the third day the men on the stick receiver's side will attack the patient's hogan, and then the patient's family will feed them and give them gifts. I tried to learn where the patient was all this time, but the young men knew only that he was treated by the medicine man after the mock battle on the third day. I would like to have asked them more questions, but they grew suspicious of me and told me that lately there had been a lot of spies around.

I wandered off by myself and watched several children play. They would lock each other in a car and then attack it. Another young man joined me. He explained that he did not know much about the dance but would try to find "some old people" who would tell me everything. He returned a few minutes later to tell me that his "uncle" was willing to talk to me. We walked over the hill to the men —many were already quite drunk—and met his "uncle," who turned out to be Harold Kennedy. Harold was very high and told me that he was glad I had found an interpreter, for there were many things he wanted to tell me.

"There are five kinds of gods in the beginning. Of these five, one made a mistake and went to the other god and killed him and then the others." Harold was almost incoherent, and my interpreter, who was not too strong in leg-

endary Navaho, was having a very hard time translating.
"There were two, who were born after the others were
killed. These two ate people. These two came from a
woman who had made a mistake with the sun. The god,
who killed the other gods, did not know about them because still another god had hidden them in a hole in the
earth. Their mother told them that they did not have a father, but they wanted to find their father anyway. 'You
can't go to your father,' the woman said. 'There are a lot
of obstacles: canyons, snakes, rocks, brambles.' The two
children decided to go anyway and on the way they found
a manhole and in the manhole Spiderman. Spiderman
gave them eagle feathers, which could lead them to their
father. And they went on, and everything their mother
had told them came true. There were a lot of pointed
rocks, bears, thunder, and sand slides. They tried to cross
the rocks and finally made it. A giant bird tried to push
them back, but they made it. They reached their father,
but he said they were not his sons. The father gave them a
pipe, but the pipe had stuff in it to kill the children. The
children put something in their mouths to prevent themselves from dying from the poison pipe. And the two sons
didn't die, and the father told them to go to his other children. The other children were rich, while the two were
real poor. They were covered with lice. They had a
Squaw Dance for the two children because there were a
lot of people who wanted to kill them—like Hopi and
white men.

"Everything else is a secret. There are many things I
could tell you, but they are secret." Thus Harold con-
cluded his bastardized version of the Hero Twins' journey
to their father, the sun.* He then asked me for two dollars, the cost of a bottle of wine. I told him I didn't have

* See the note on the origin legend of Enemy Way on p. 237.

it and gave him a dollar, the first money I had given an informant. Harold thanked me and started off and then turned around and staggered back.

"I want you to know," he said, "that they say I have killed a man at the Pow-Wow. I want you to be my friend and not afraid of me. You must know that I have not killed anyone." Harold looked me directly in the eye and shook my hand long and firmly. I knew he hadn't committed the murder. Drunk as he was, he would never have shaken my hand—in the white man's way—had he been guilty.

As I returned to the arbor I noticed that Cora was still in the car. She must have been there for three or four hours now. Forster was eating blood sausages, which, I learned, are prepared by stuffing the stomach of a sheep with a mixture of blood and corn meal and a little fat and then boiling it until it turns brick-red. I tasted it and found it not unlike overcooked *andouillette*. The stick receiver came up and asked Forster who I was, and when Forster had completed a rather lengthy explanation, he shook my hands solemnly and told me that as a friend of the Navaho I was welcome.

By four thirty there were perhaps two hundred people awaiting the arrival of the patient and his party. The women were in traditional clothes and wore, for the most part, white socks and sneakers, moccasins, or saddle shoes. One woman was in a black velveteen blouse with quarters sewn up the sleeves to her elbows. I offered to drive Martha and Cora, who wanted to change, back to Little Bluff, but Forster refused. A few minutes later, however, he tried to persuade me to accept from a friend a Japanese transistor radio as pawn, and when I said that I had no money, he suggested I go to the trading post to cash a check. Although I had no intention of doing this I agreed.

I was anxious to get a sweater for the all-night vigil. It had become quite chilly, and rain clouds were settling in over us.

As we started off down the dirt road that leads to the highway, we were forced to the side by three or four horsemen followed by seven or eight pickup trucks draped with yarn and stuffed with shouting Navahos. This was the patient's party. I later learned that the night before there had been a ceremony at the patient's camp. Here, after a drum has been made and the items necessary for the preparation of the prayer stick have been placed in a basket in the center of the ceremonial hogan, women of the clan which is arranging the dance, as well as friends and relatives, both male and female, bring yarn—a symbol of their desire to participate in the ceremony. After the prayer stick is finally accepted by the stick receiver, the yarn is given to the women of the stick receiver's side who will use it in weaving rugs or for tassels on saddle blankets.

I was sorry to have missed the stick receiver's acceptance of the prayer stick. The patient's party had arrived early—at five o'clock instead of sundown. By the time I had turned the car around and returned, the prayer stick had been inspected, accepted, and confided to the young virgin whose responsibility it was for the duration of the dance. I was told that she was only nine or ten because they couldn't find any older girls who were still virgins. The stick receiver's party was busy feeding the patient's party. I noticed that the two sides ate separately. Martha, Cora, and I went to Little Bluff, and when we returned, it was raining hard—the first real rain I had seen on the reservation—and what had been a scene of festivity and color was now bedraggled and gray. Everyone was soaked and trembling with cold except for a few older Navahos who had been fortunate enough to bring Pendleton blankets, which they wore as ponchos. The rain and cold were an excellent excuse for drinking. Fight was in the air.

No one really knew when the singing and dancing would begin. I talked to several young men, who were wearing army jackets and had "come to see the girls." They did not even know who the patient and the stick receiver were. A tall Navaho with a very large pocked nose —the only Navaho con man I ever met—told me that he had had a college education and was a famous artist. When I asked him if he had ever had a Squaw Dance, he told me that he hadn't because he didn't believe in the Navaho religion. Then he announced that he was a medicine man and took out several feathered sticks, which he pressed against my head and chest, and shouted evangelical prayers. He claimed to be a hand trembler and stargazer and unwrapped a piece of crystal from his pouch. "Hide a dollar anywhere you want on you," he said. "If I find out with this here magic crystal where it is, I keep it. If not, I give you a dollar." A crowd had gathered around, and when I asked him to show me his dollar first, he grew hurt and told me I had no faith. He pressed his prayer sticks against me and shouted more prayers "to Our Holy Father to teach this white sinner faith in the power of God" and then tried the same stunt. Again I insisted on seeing the dollar first, but this time, before he had a chance to convince me, one of the Navaho boys in the military jacket told him he had hidden a quarter. The artist–medicine man started mumbling in Navaho and English with an occasional French word thrown in.

I never saw the result. Harry had come to tell me that Forster was looking for me. I found him in the car with Cora, Martha, Joan Shepard, and a friend. Forster was drunk. He had just given Joan a pint of wine, which she finished off before he could stop her, and now was lecturing the girls—half in English, half in Navaho. It appeared that although Forster wanted to go home, the girls wanted to stay for the dance. He would not hear of this. All they would do was to get in trouble and have to quit school. By the time I got in the car, it was settled. Forster and his daughters were leaving. Joan and her friend could do whatever they liked. They stayed.

When we got to Little Bluff, Forster insisted that Martha and Cora prepare hot corn and coffee to warm us up. When the meal was served he called them into the kitchen, lined them up against the wall, and harangued them. Education was the most important thing in life, he stated. They should not run around because it was not good. It was bad for education. You had to make sacrifices for good things. . . . Forster repeated himself again and again and every minute or so would turn to me for confirmation. Finally after five or ten minutes, I told him I thought the girls had understood. "Do you understand what I am saying?" Forster asked and, much to my surprise, Cora said she didn't. She was obviously siding with her father despite his drunken anger. Forster continued. Once when he was in the sixth grade he was punished for reading a funny book in class. His teacher twisted his arm and took him to the principal. He felt very bad and apologized and was still punished. He had to work that weekend. He never brought in another comic book. It was this lesson that made him what he is. He won three sweaters: a three-striper, which Rita still has, for basketball, a two-striper for running, and a one-striper for being a generally well-rounded student.

Forster then talked about his army life. After he had been in Texas for a short time, he received a furlough and returned to the reservation to marry their mother. "Up until then we was just friends." He then told them about how he had been busted in Pennsylvania. He had a *white* girl friend, who made him come home with her, and whenever he wanted to leave she said, "Don't leave, Honey. You're a good piece of Japanese ass." He made love to her two or three times. When their mother asked him why he was busted he told her that he was late in returning from New York. She sent him money in Seattle, and there he picked up a Shoshone girl. "Baby, I'm lonely and I love you," he told her. "I put my hand around her, and she said she loved soldier boys," Forster blustered. "We walked around and around and made love. We went dancing and drank a little bit and made love everywhere, even off crowded street in alley. When I had to leave, she cried and cried and cried and said not to go. I receive one letter from her in Hawaii, but I never answer. I had a lot of fighting to do. She say she didn't like any man but me."

Forster, who had lost the point of his lecture, continued to recount his war experiences. Cora and Martha sneaked out of the room. I asked him where he had gotten the tattoo on his left shoulder.

"I got it in Okinawa on day war ended. It was made by Japanese person. A lot of girls, they kiss it. Gosh, I had a lot of girls. Japanese girls, especially in Hawaii."

He remained silent for a few minutes and then asked me to help him write a letter to Sally. He dictated the following:

Dear Sally,

I am writing to you tonight a special letter to find out how you are getting along with your job there. Everybody was saying that your position in Wayne is very bad. I am sorry to write this to you.

I want to remind you how much I have helped you while you were in school. I have been good to you and have helped

*you whenever you asked and in whatever way I could. Now
that you have been working for several months you should
have enough money to pay me back what I lent you for merchandise and groceries. I need this money for the Ford pickup
which I want to buy next year.*

*I do not say that I don't like you. I still like you better than
anybody else. But you had better make up your mind what
you want to do. You can pay me back the money personally.
If you do not pay it back, I will write to your boss. If this
does not work, then I will have to go to the Navaho Tribal
Court. I have already talked to the judge in Window Rock.
He said that I would have to ask you for the money first before a court order is possible. To go to the Navaho court
would cost money. You would have to pay a court fee of fifty
dollars, and I would have to pay the judge twenty-five dollars.
I would like it better to settle this personally and not go to
the Tribe, but if you do not agree, I will not hesitate.*

*I have given you over one hundred fifty dollars, and if you
repay me quickly you will only have to pay one hundred dollars. If you do not like this, come to see me, and we will talk
things over ourselves. Then I would not have to see you in the
Tribal Court.*

*I hope you are getting along well. We all miss you here. I
hope you change your way of life and come back here. We all
like you and your people very much. Good-bye. Good luck. I
hope to hear from you soon.*

Forster

As Forster dictated this, Harry came in and listened. At
the end Forster asked me to make five copies for him. He
told me that his relatives don't approve of Sally. "I don't
know what's wrong with that girl. I just don't understand," he said and shook his head sadly.

JULY 30

EVERYONE WOKE UP LATE. John, who had been on a school trip to Carteret, had returned in time to go to the Squaw Dance. He told us that there had been several fights and that Lana had stopped by late. She hasn't been home in several days, and Forster, who was becoming a little anxious, asked me to go with John and Harry to fetch her. We tried several homes before we finally found her at a girl friend's. She looked hung-over and smiled her knowing smile as she asked me to stop at a (boy) friend's house, where she had left something. When we got back to Little Bluff, everyone was ready to go to Carteret. Forster planned to spend the night. He was due back at work August 1.

Steven Foster's camp looked deserted. Two of his neighbors had gone off to Utah the day before yesterday to work as pickers, and Steven himself was waiting for a truck to take him to Mines, where he intended to go to a peyote meeting. He seemed very distracted. "They will tell me what to do," he said completely out of context and would not explain himself. He walked off, and when I started to jot down a comment, he came back and looked at my notes suspiciously to see whether I had mentioned peyote. I told him I hadn't and tried to make conversation, but it was useless. I asked him to help me by making a map of Little Bluff, but he refused. "The police won't allow it," he said. I insisted, explaining that I wanted him to make a map because I knew him and had confidence in him. "If you know me, then you know that the truck comes soon to pick me up," he said irritably and walked off. In fact, he was still waiting for it two hours later.

A rather good-looking woman in her late twenties dressed in blue jeans—one of the few women I've seen here in pants—was frying potatoes and onions in a nearby cabin, which I had never visited. It had always been empty. She was very friendly and told me that, as both she and her husband worked, they were rarely at home. She had finished the eleventh grade and was a teaching assistant at a local high school. Her husband, who had completed high school and a course in surveying, worked for the Highway Department. He was due back any minute and would be better able to answer my questions because he grew up in the area. She had moved to Little Bluff when they were married, because he had a job here.

Greg Shaw was in fact most helpful. Not only did he give me a full genealogy, but when he was not sure of a point, he would ask his mother, who lived in a neighboring hogan. His map of Little Bluff was "professional." He was the only Navaho who included physical features and all of the hogans. He told me that he had no intention of moving off the reservation because he could earn more money here. He is hired by the job at $2.98 per hour and has just been laid off for a week or so. When I asked him if he had any sheep, he answered, "No, I don't have anything except what's here"—he pointed to his head— "only education." He had a collegiate air about him.

Greg had not been to the Squaw Dance. He had heard that there had been some fighting—someone had even pulled a knife—but he was not surprised. "It happens all the time," he said. He himself didn't know anything about this particular dance; he wasn't related to either party. Tonight would be the biggest night of all. "Navaho from all over would come around." Everyone would bring his own food, but the patient would supply firewood and water. There would be a lot of dancing.

Forster returned at six thirty. He was drunk and had decided not to spend the night in Carteret but to go to the second night of the Squaw Dance. I drove Lana to a girl friend's to pick up some groceries, which she had left by mistake. The two girls gossiped in English for a half hour. It sounded like typical high-school gossip, but I wasn't sure what the expressions designated. Did "to go with" mean, for example, "to sleep with"? When we returned, everyone was ready to go to the dance. Without apologizing for not taking me, they all left, but an hour later Forster returned alone with Harry Young. The children had decided to go to a western dance instead, and Forster had come back to take me to the Squaw Dance. He was very angry at his children and locked the house so they couldn't get in. He even nailed the back door shut.

When we arrived at nine thirty, over a hundred cars and trucks were parked in a huge circle. Around a fire in the center between six and twelve singers—their number varied through the night—sang away in falsetto. As the evening progressed, the singers split into two groups, each with a drum, and began to sing competitively. At one time they improvised in English: "Raise her up. Raise my baby up. . . . Let her down. Let my baby down." I tried to determine the composition of the two competing groups and was told that one group represented the people on the patient's side and the other people on the stick receiver's side. "People" were not just relatives but friends as well. I had the impression that the composition of the two groups was in fact quite informal. Both sides tried to recruit me, and I sang with both, moving from side to side without any difficulty. When I asked one of the singers why they were competing, he told me it was the best way to stay awake.

Many of the older people went to sleep in the cars and trucks. Boys and girls strolled around the outer rim of cars. Even though the girls moved in groups of two or three, the boys attempted to pick them up without much success, from what I could see. The Navaho police, who had come to keep peace, ignored the men and occasional women who could be seen drinking on the sly. No one seemed to know when the dancing would begin or where the patient was. One young man suggested he was at his camp with the medicine man. I could not even find the virgin with the prayer stick. By two o'clock most people realized that there would be no dancing and had gone to sleep. I wandered around groggily for another half hour, wondering what had brought all these people together for such a boring event. Everyone really knew that the girls preferred community-center dances and weren't about to ask a group of drunken, bellicose men to dance. Finally I fell asleep in the back of Forster's car.

JULY 31

THE SINGING ENDED at daybreak. Within a half hour most of the cars and trucks had pulled off, but Forster insisted that we remain at the second night's camp for a couple of hours to give the patient's party time to prepare for the arrival of their guests. He said that most of the spectators would not go to the patient's camp. "They didn't belong."

When we got to the camp, which was about twenty minutes away, women were still preparing breakfast and a man on horseback was shouting directions, which were generally ignored. "He is telling the people what to do," one man told me. "He tells them to follow the ways of the old people, to remember that this a religious occasion and not a social one. They should think of the sick woman." His exhortations reminded me of one ethnologist's comment on South American tribal leaders: everyone listens and then does as he pleases. My informant told me that the Squaw Dance was given for a woman who "keeps falling down." Evidently she had fainting spells and convulsions. She had spent the night, he assured me, in the ceremonial hogan with the medicine man. Later I caught a glimpse of her seated alone on the northwest side of the ceremonial hogan, lost in herself. She was a middle-aged woman. I was not able to talk to her because she was supposed to keep aloof. My informant did not know her relation to the man whose camp we were at, but knew that she was from the general area and a member of the same clan, *Deschini*. He thought she might be his sister. The stick receiver belongs to the *Todachini* clan.

Forster called me over to have breakfast. He had already managed to have a few drinks. We sat down under the crowded arbor and dipped fried bread into greasy mutton soup. Forster was consuming an enormous quantity of soup and finally said something in Navaho that made everyone laugh.

"He's drinking a lot of soup," my neighbor translated, "because it'll give him a big hard-on."

Forster then picked up the pot of soup and downed the remainder without stopping for breath. He was quite a sight: his hair was disheveled, his eyes yellow and bloodshot, his mouth and chin greasy, and his nylon shirt covered with dribble.

After breakfast everyone stood around awaiting the arrival of the stick receiver and the attack on the ceremonial hogan. Finally we heard a few shouts, and four or five men, including the stick receiver, rode into camp and cir- cled the ceremonial hogan several times. I do not think they "attacked" it four times, as tradition requires. I was very disappointed. The mock battle seemed a very paltry affair indeed.

The men dismounted and joined the other members of their party, who were already awaiting the arrival of the food under a large arbor built especially for the occasion about a hundred fifty yards east of the ceremonial hogan. Steaming platters of mutton—we had only had soup— were soon carried to the guests, who had gathered in fam- ily groups.

A man in his late sixties, who spoke fluent English—he had been an interpreter for several anthropologists— joined me and explained that in a few minutes the stick receiver's people would gather around the hogan to re- ceive gifts. "First they give gifts and then they get them. It's like a seesaw," he observed.

As we were waiting for the exchange, he told me that things had sure changed. "This here area used to be des- ert," he remarked. "There wasn't a hogan in miles. Now look at it. Everywhere you turn there's a hogan." I looked around and could see no other camp for miles. Indeed, the area seemed especially desolate.

"There are a lot of white men who want to learn Nav- aho ways," my informant said, changing the subject. "I've known several myself. There's the son of a trader down at Red Circle who's more Navaho than white. He speaks the language better than me. He's married to a Navaho girl."

Although a few packages were still being delivered to the ceremonial hogan, people on the stick receiver's side had started to gather in front of it. My informant explained that not only people on the patient's side but those on the stick receiver's side contribute gifts. "They give the patient a hand. A Squaw Dance costs a lot of money." As we were calculating how many sheep had been consumed for breakfast, the people in front of the hogan began to sing the four Coyote songs. I was told that they have no real meaning but "just sound like coyotes." By the time they were finished, about forty or fifty people had gathered in front of the hogan in no particular order. The stick receiver was prominent in their midst. At some distance from the crowd were the spectators who were either members of the patient's family or outsiders. In the area between the two groups were a few of the spectators' children, irresistibly drawn to the crowd and the presents.

As some of the sway songs I had heard the night before were being sung, a barrage of popcorn, candy, Cracker Jacks, dime-store toys, and cigarettes were thrown out of the smoke hole. Everyone reached in a mad jumble for the gifts, and just as they settled back content or disappointed, a second barrage, and then a third, shot out. Larger gifts—bolts of calico, sacks of potatoes, and even a sheep—were handed out through the hogan door, probably to specific individuals. At the very end there was a commotion. I couldn't see what was happening, but my informant told me that the stick receiver's drummer had just given up his drum. He explained that there were two drums, one for each side, and now the patient's side had them both.

Everyone moved off and settled in the shade. It was after nine. A group of older men were smoking under a sun shade in front of the ceremonial hogan and would not let me near. "It's secret," they told me. "The medicine man's with the sick woman." Several white men arrived. One, a trader, started to argue with two Navaho men, and within five minutes what rapport I had established was completely lost. The white people formed a knot of outsiders. Whenever I asked a question about the dance, I was told it was secret. Two young men informed me that they had been watching me carefully and were preparing a report which they were going to send to Window Rock. I went off in search of Forster and found him in a sheepfold with two cronies. The three men were drunk and dirty.

"What you want?" Forster asked.

"I came to find out where you were."

"What you want to know that for?" he slurred.

"Because I want to know when you are leaving," I answered.

"Sometime. Don't *you* worry. I tell you ahead of time. Do *you* understand?"

I said I did and sat down. Forster asked me if I had any money. I told him I didn't.

"I just thought you want a drink, only two dollars," he explained.

Forster suddenly staggered to his feet and walked over to a woman in her late thirties and three men who were fishing in their pockets for change, which they gave her. She produced from under her blouse a pint of whiskey, which they consumed in less than two minutes. I timed them. A young man, with whom I had been talking earlier, asked them for a drink but was too late. He was followed by two thirteen-year-old girls dressed in black ski pants. Forster tried to goose one of them, but she pushed him away and started to talk to my friend.

"These girls here ask you who you are," he said drunkenly. "They want to go in the shadows with you."

I shrugged my shoulders, and they walked off with my

friend, who returned two or three minutes later.

"I was sick," he burped.

Forster waddled over to a second sheep pen and plopped down next to a toothless old hag and began to woo her. Everyone turned to watch. She smiled flirtatiously, and Forster squeezed her chin and whispered something in her ear. He then took her hand—she blushed—but dropped it the moment he caught sight of a friend, who he thought had some wine.

I wandered off by myself. I was tired and bored and very irritable. There was nothing I could do. Even though the trader had left without a fight, no one wanted to talk to me. They were either too drunk or too resentful or both. After all, what right did I, a white man, have to be here in the middle of a ceremony designed to cure a woman of foreign contact—most probably white contact? Had I found any true interest or concern in the religious aspect of the ceremony, this argument would have made sense, but it seemed evident that most of the Navahos did not know what was going on and didn't really care. The ritual had become hollow, meaningless, a lame excuse to break the boredom of welfare life. Had the white man done this? I remembered reading about the Navaho captives at Fort Sumner who used to ride broomsticks the two hundred feet from one camp to another at their Squaw Dances because they had to go on horseback and there were no horses. I wondered what effect these "hollow" rites would have on the patient and then realized that there was probably more to Forster's not having a Squaw Dance to free himself from the burden of all those dead Japanese and Americans he had seen and buried. The conflict wasn't between "modern ways" and "Navaho ways," neither of which he was part of, as I had thought too simply, but rather between marginal modern and moribund Navaho ways. In the end, I supposed, there was no choice.

Harry, who had been sleeping in the car, came to tell me that Forster wanted to go and led me to the cooking arbor, where he was drinking more mutton soup. After fifteen or twenty minutes of drunken indecision on Forster's part, Harry and I piled him and another drunk into the car and drove off. When we got back to Little Bluff, we found Forster's daughters in front of the house. They had spent the night under the arbor and looked peevish, though not angry, as I would have expected. They joined us as we delivered our drunk to his family.

AUGUST 1

FORSTER WENT BACK TO WORK this morning and returned at lunch to find out whether I had finished his letter to Sally. I hadn't. He had gone back to the Squaw Dance later yesterday afternoon because Joan Shepard, Sally's sister and Forster's friend from the Pow-Wow, had asked him. She is much more forward than any of Forster's children.

"Joan, she dance with me," Forster said proudly. "We all come back real late, maybe two, maybe three o'clock in the morning. Work doesn't go with sleepy head. Gosh, all the girls tease me at work."

At six o'clock Forster returned from work—over two hours late. Today he had to substitute for another maintenance man, who was suffering from a gall-bladder infection.

"I had bad gall bladder too," he remarked. "Big operation. I stay in hospital twelve days. Then they give me month to rest. Rest and recuperation. Insurance pay for loan from finance company. That was real nice. They pay three times. They give me loan just on credit. Car paid in full. Just credit."

"I never go to Squaw Dance again," Forster announced at dinner. "Too dirty. Too much running around. Me and friend, we drink two pints at dance and then he get in big fight. . . ." Forster had not gotten involved.

"A lot of people dance," he continued. "Everybody had boy friend—Martha, Joan, Cora, not Helen." Helen, who lives at Dan Shepard's and is about sixteen, and Joan were both at dinner. "Helen, she different. She stay in car." The girls blushed.

"Did you have a girl friend?" Lana asked her father maliciously.

"No," Forster answered, and then changing the subject, told his daughter how I had to stay up nearly all the first night of the dance because Harold Kennedy was in the back seat of the car. "He sure take up a lot of room— whole back seat. He snore so loud that I couldn't finish my dream. I dream about Rita.

"We had to look all over for Martha," Forster added a few minutes later. Martha lowered her eyes, and Lana exaggerated her surprise.

"I'd never go to a Squaw Dance," she said superciliously, looked at her sister, and laughed.

After dinner I read Forster his letter to Sally. He seemed satisfied. I asked him if he thought she would give him back the money.

"I don't know," he said, and after a pause—"I don't think so. She has money though. She always goes to dances here."

"Does she send money home?" I asked.

"I don't know. I don't think so. Nobody ever says that Sally give them money."

Forster sat in silence for a few minutes.

"I hope she doesn't get mad," he said at last. "The letter is good—not too strong. Maybe she come back here. Then she wouldn't have to pay." He laughed. "She knows about it. You know that boy, her brother, he talked to her about it. I don't think she believe me."

"The letter will show her that you are serious," I said.

"Umm. You know that man who came here a few days ago in green pickup," Forster said, referring to a friend who had stopped by several days ago to say hello. "Well, he seen her two weeks ago at dance. She always has money for dance. Last week there was a dance at Nugget. . . ." Forster assumed, without really knowing, that Sally had been there. "She always need money. Every time she comes here, she ask me for money. Last time, twenty dollars. Time before, twenty dollars. That's a lot of money. Forty dollars. When I see her in Wayne, there is never any groceries there. I give her dishes, cups, spoons, plates, forks. It cost me nearly twenty dollars. That's a lot of money."

"Do you have any papers?" I asked.

"No, I just have it in my account book," he answered. "She probably say that her father pay. I don't like that. He doesn't work."

Forster sat thinking to himself.

"You know that girl Helen. She is good girl," he mused.

"Is she Harry's sister?" I asked.

"Yes, his real sister. Her name is Young too. I don't know why they have name Young. Maybe father he come from Frontier. People have that name there. Helen, she never leave car at dance. Don't run around."

"She lives at Dan Shepard's, doesn't she?"

"Yes, I don't know why. All the kids of that mother they come around. Always lots of kids."

"Harry is a good boy," I remarked.

"Not good," Forster contradicted. "He hangs around too much. The mother she come around and ask me where he is. Not good to take him around."

"Did he come back from the Squaw Dance with you?"

"No," Forster answered. "He eats here. Cost a lot of money."

"At least he works hard," I suggested. Forster has in fact been using Harry as a handyman. He has washed the car several times and made minor repairs around the house. I was surprised to hear Forster talk this way. He usually shows a great deal of affection for Harry.

"Gosh, I'm tired," Forster yawned. "Nearly fall asleep. Two hours overtime. I didn't want to go back to dance but Joan want to. She take my hand."

He grew silent.

"Lots of fights there," he said sleepily. "No police. I never go again."

AUGUST 2

LAST NIGHT THERE WAS a thunderstorm nearby, and at breakfast Forster remarked three times that there had been lightning.

"It scare me," he said.

After dinner, as I was sitting alone in front of the house, Martha silently handed me a letter. It was from her brother in Germany and read something like this:

This has been a long time since I wrote to you there. Here everything is in good condition as the Army is. The weather here is fine, rain this morning. A little cold sometimes, but here the weather sometimes changes. I hope the weather there is fine and the crops. A big hello to you and the kids.

As for the Army here, it has been fine lately. I don't believe I have been in the Army this long, but I'm getting short, about six months more to go.

Most of the past months we have been out in the field and will be going out again. This will be this coming month. . . . There not much news around here. Theres going to be a parade this coming Friday for the change of command in our battalion. Most of the time in the field we have been assign to an Armor Battalion. This is for the new field training coming up next month.

There not much news around here and thank Cora and Martha for the nice wonderful letters. Enjoyed reading them, will drop them a post card later. Also tell Rita and Lana to write. Thanks and a big hello again.

Answer soon.

I was very touched. It was the first time that Martha had ever acknowledged my presence in more than a mechanical way. I felt a member of the family.

Later Forster asked me to help him draft an answer to his son. He seemed at a loss for words, but Dan Shepard, who had stopped by, urged him on, suggesting he mention his vacation and the Squaw Dance. The following letter was finally arrived at.

Dear Son,

I got your letter yesterday. It has been a long time since I have had a letter from you. I was very glad to hear from you and to know how you have been getting along in the army. We are glad that you will be returning for discharge in six months. You are very lucky that you will be discharged before China starts to fight.

Here at home everything is fine. I'm still working at the same place. I just finished one month of vacation—the whole of July. I went back to work on August 1. The kids are doing fine. They are all here. All of them say hello and will write you. Rita has been working in Grand Canyon all summer. John and Lana have summer jobs in town. Martha and Cora do nothing but housework. They cook in the morning and evening. Soon everybody is going back to school.

The weather is not too bad but dry. There has not been enough rain. Nobody has raised corn because there is no water. It is too hot.

Rita is going back to school on the nineteenth of August. Cora is going back this month. Lana goes back to Albuquerque at the end of the month. Rita and Lana graduate this year. John and Martha are still in school in town. There will only be the three of us here next month.

There is no other news. Write us how you are getting along in the army in your next letter.

There are a lot of Squaw Dances going on.

Lucille and Harold Kennedy send a big hello. They are still here. Dan Shepard is sitting right next to me. He says hello. Everybody is fine in Little Bluff.

I'm closing the letter now. No more news until next time. Good-bye. God bless you everywhere you might be.

Love,
Forster

I was surprised that he made no mention of me.

AUGUST 3

"JOAN SHEPARD she caught with a man," Forster said at dinner. "She caught at Squaw Dance up here in town. Police take her back to her father. She was very drunk. Police say that if they catch her again they throw her in jail. She is in sheep camp with her mother now."

"They can't do that," John interrupted. "She is only seventeen. She can't be arrested."

"Maybe they arrest father then," Forster suggested.

"Police can't throw father in jail," John argued. "He didn't do anything wrong."

"He responsible for her," Forster answered. "He is father."

Forster and John continued the argument in Navaho. I was surprised to hear John take such a vehement stand and wondered what vested interest he had in proving his point.

"It not good for kids to run around," Forster said, switching back into English. "Too much drinking for kids. Police say she very drunk."

Forster had evidently forgotten that it was he who had given Joan a pint of wine the night she was arrested.

AUGUST 4

COLIN CURTIS WAS READING a newspaper when I arrived at his place this morning. He explained that he gets a lot of newspapers from his wife, who works in a restaurant, and then asked me about a mass murder he had read about. He could not understand why anyone would want to kill.

When I told him that I had been to the Squaw Dance —he had not been able to go—and didn't understand what was going on, he immediately sat down at his table under the arbor and began a careful explanation of the ceremony. He seemed troubled by the fact that I had not understood.

"You have to put off the Squaw Dance if a relative dies," he began. He was referring to the Squaw Dance which was supposed to have been held in the area but was postponed twice: first because the prayer stick had broken on the way to the stick receiver's and second because a relative of the patient had drowned. There has been much talk about this in Little Bluff.

"You have a Squaw Dance if you have killed a white man or if you've killed someone in war," he continued. "This bothers you when you come back. You have bad dreams. You can't sleep. This is one way to have a Squaw Dance. It's also necessary to have enough money to give the dance. Relatives help by bringing food. A lot of people are necessary. They have to haul food, water, and wood. Some people don't have enough money or enough relatives. They just have to do without it."

"Did you ever have a Squaw Dance?" I asked.

"No," Colin answered and added noncommittally, "Some people don't believe in Squaw Dances."

"First it is necessary to make a feather stick," he continued. "Then the relatives of the sick person come around and sing and all come into the hogan about ten o'clock at night to decide where they are going to go, who will get the feather stick.

"Sometimes a man and a wife have a Squaw Dance. Then a boy sits between them. He must carry the feather stick to the people. Then they go—if they have horses they go in a straight line, if they have a car, they go by road—to the receiver's camp. They have bought yarn, which they put on their cars and horses. The boy carries the feather stick. The husband and wife are the patients and come along. If one of them is too sick, he stays at home. They must be very careful with the stick. They have to arrive by four or five o'clock. They can rest on the way if they want to. By afternoon everything is ready at the receiver's place."

Colin interrupted himself to explain that the stick receiver had been forewarned. According to Colin he had been chosen by the patient's party largely on the basis of wealth. Once he has been informed, the stick receiver must be prepared to accept the feather stick in a day or two. Never three, Colin assured me. "It is bad for him to refuse the stick unless there has been a death in the family.

"About ten in the morning," Colin continued, "they start to take the feather stick. When they come close to the receiver's camp, they put yarn on the cars and horses. The man who gets the stick has to be in his hogan. He checks the stick to see if it is good. If it is not good, he gives it back. They take it over the hill to fix it. This happened a couple of years ago in town. If the stick is good, the women on the receiver's side run out to the cars and horses and grab the yarn and bring it back."

The patient is then led under a specially constructed arbor where he and his family eat. The others eat later. Colin was careful to specify that the people on the patient's side eat apart from those on the stick receiver's side.

"In the evening they start to sing. The receiver is the leader of the songs. He rests sometimes. About three they have the dance and at five or six they knock off the dance. Nowadays they dance only two or three hours."

In the morning, after breakfast and the gift exchange, the members of the patient's party leave for their own camp to prepare for the arrival of their guests the following morning. The latter leave in the afternoon and spend the night not too far from the patient's camp. The patient is in his hogan and should not hear the singing.

"In the afternoon they bring wood and water to this camp and then they go back to their camp. Some of the people stay. There is singing and dancing. You shouldn't dance with a close relative. Girls don't go much to Squaw Dances any more. The old sentiments die away. In the old days a lot of people danced.

"The feather stick has to be watched all the time to make sure it is not damaged." Earlier Colin explained that it was guarded by a virgin girl or boy. I had never heard of a boy stick carrier.

"In the morning around six thirty, the people go to the sick person's camp. An arbor has been made for them. Nearby is a shed for the medicine stuff."

Colin described the breakfast and gift exchange. "The receiver gets expensive gifts—maybe a cow or a horse or two sheep." Forster has told me that sheep sell for about sixteen dollars on the reservation.

"The patient has been up all night with the medicine man," Colin continued. "A lot of people go over the hill and shoot and kill the devils." Presumably he was referring to the symbolic slaying of the enemy ghost who had been haunting the patient. A trophy from the tribe of the ghost in the form of bones or, formerly, a scalp is shot by an old man and strewn with ashes. "Then the patient is painted black. If a person believes he will be killed in the Squaw Dance, he can get a little paint and put it on his face." Colin did not mention the patient's killing the ghost by thrusting a crow's beak at the trophy.

"In the afternoon they can have clowns. They make fun of the people. It is not necessary to have them. The clowns chase people but cannot go into the [ceremonial] hogan. They dig a big hole which they fill with water and make mud. The last time I went to a Squaw Dance there were six clowns. Somebody has to carry a special medicine for the clowns in case they fall so that they will not lose consciousness. Before the clowns there is singing and afterward people go into the sweat house to clean up. Then there is more singing and dancing. In the morning it is all over. Some people hang around. The receiver carries the feather stick away. He takes it apart and hides it."

When he had finished his description, which had lasted well over an hour, I asked Colin if there was a story behind the dance. His version, which follows, is an even greater distortion of the original legend than Harold Kennedy's, but unlike Harold, Colin apologized for having forgotten most of it.

"It begins way back. There were two boys. I think they were twins but I don't remember. They were the ones who killed the devils. I don't remember how they killed them. One, I remember, was a big giant man. There was also a big elephant. The boys tried to visit the sun, but they couldn't get there. One of the gods told them that they could not go there because their father would kill them. The boys began to die. Then they had a Squaw Dance to prevent themselves from dying. This was the first Squaw Dance."

"Did the boys ever get to the sun?" I asked.

"No, they never made it," he answered, thus neatly reversing the outcome of the original legend of the Hero Twins' perilous but successful journey to their father, the sun.* "One of the giants," he added, "turned into petrified wood.

"Changing Woman, the mother of the boys," he recalled, "lay below a spring and water dripped into her.

* See the note on the origin legend of Enemy Way on p. 237.

She was looking up at the sun then and got pregnant."

He sat back, tired. "I can't remember the stories," he said sadly. "Maybe someday I get a tape recorder and record all my father's stories. I try writing them down once, but it didn't work.

"You know," he started after a long pause, "sometimes sun and moon cause people to die. . . ." He never finished his thought.

"Do you dream much?" I asked, after a few minutes of silence.

"No, not much," he answered. "How would you feel if you dreamed you were going to die?"

"It would bother me," I replied.

"It wouldn't bother me," Colin explained, "because I believe in God. If I dream that somebody else dies, who is not of my clan or a relation, then I have nothing to do with it. Maybe my mother has dream that her husband will die. She worries and goes to a medicine man. He does something so that her husband doesn't die. Of course someday I will die myself. That is the way it has to be."

A long silence.

"I dream that I die last night," Colin said at last. "My mother might worry about me. But it has to be. It was just a dream. If you have sheep, then you have to give them to the medicine man. My mother told me if you have a dream like that you have to do something. When you tell the old people Bible stories, they say they are just like ours. It is hard to make people believe."

It was not until I returned to my hogan and began to look through my notes that I realized how troubled Colin was. His monotone had masked his concern and anxiety.

Before leaving, I asked him about an old rock formation I had seen on the way to Window Rock.

"Once there were all kinds of snakes," Colin answered.

"People were sitting on a snake to see where it would go. The snake crawled to a place and curled up and made a big lake where water cannot leave. The snake stayed there for a night and the next day it crawled on. Two people were left behind. Somebody had to go back and get them. Two people went back and saw that the two had been turned into rock. The people returned to the snake and the snake went on to Red Mountain, where it made a rainbow. It went on further, but I don't remember where. The people used the snake for transportation."

"One day Mormons come here," Forster said at dinner, "right here in this place. I tell them, 'I come here in 1936. Then there was only Presbyterian.' 'You ought to believe me,' they say. I tell them that Christ said that we must believe Him and not you, not just a man, Joseph Smith. The Mormons compete with other churches. They steal other members. Presbyterian believe in Christ. Catholics, like Mormons. They don't pray to Christ but to Mary. But they better than Mormons. I think they good in education."

"What about Baptists?" I asked.

"Just like Presbyterians," Forster answered. "They are lower though because they scare you. They tell you, you burn in hell if you sin. Presbyterians say that it is not necessary to scare people." And then confidentially he added, "Mormons run around with women. They get people by coming and saying, 'You need to go to the market, you need firewood. Come, we take you.' That is how they get people. Now there are too many churches in town."

AUGUST 5

AFTER DINNER Forster, John, the girls, and
I all went out to finish the fence. Forster had almost sin-
gle-handedly put in all the posts in their new places. We
strung the wire and bolted in the wagon wheels to form a
gate.

"Howard Lightfoot sure like wagon wheels," Forster
said, stepping back to admire his work. "What you
think?"

I told him the wheels looked beautiful.

"We paint posts white," he suggested. "I have paint in
shed. Plenty white paint. Wheels will be red. Payday I
buy special red paint, the kind that comes in cans with
button, and we paint them."

We all nodded our approval. Martha, Cora, and even
Lana joined John, who had already gone to fetch the
white paint. I had never seen Forster's children so enthu-
siastic, or so admiring of their father. They painted until
well after dark.

AUGUST 6

FORSTER FINISHED PAINTING the fence early
in the morning.

Greg Shaw bicycled over on his Moulton later to borrow some .30-30 ammunition. He wanted to have a little
target practice. Harold Kennedy had told him Forster had

some. The two men talked for a while, mostly in Navaho, about animals. When Forster finally gave him the ammunition, he was careful to tell him that it was worth about five dollars.

At lunch John suddenly blurted out that he would like to get his hands on that book I was writing. He accused me of being a spy. Forster got angry and told John that he was too smart for his own good and that if he didn't watch out he'd end up just like Desmond Bell, who wanders around without any money. After John left, Forster told me not to worry about him. He doesn't know what he's talking about. I wasn't sure. John seems more and more resentful of me lately. He probably feels that in some way I have usurped his place.

After lunch Forster and I took his old transmission to town to be rebuilt in case he has any more trouble. On the way back we passed a group of horseback riders carrying a prayer stick to Mines, where there is to be another Squaw Dance. We followed them for a few miles and then stopped to inspect a mountain spring. Forster did not know any of the families involved in the dance and did not plan to go.

When we returned to Little Bluff, Forster suddenly announced that as soon as Lana returned he was leaving for Carteret. He had originally intended to go tomorrow, and Lana, who did not know of his change of plans, had gone off with some friends for the afternoon. Forster waited for her to return—he somehow expected her to know of his imminent departure—he grew more and more irritated.

"Lana run around too much," he said. "She all over the place. Never at home. Too many boy friends. Too many girl friends. Boy friends used to come around all the time. Even in the middle of the night. I tell them to get out or

I shoot them. Maybe I do same with girl friends."

After having waited about a half hour, Forster finally left with Cora and John. Martha had quietly gone off earlier in the day for a week at a Baptist camp. As he was leaving, Forster asked me to make sure the house was locked—otherwise, Lana would bring all her girl friends over—and tell her to spend the night in town. When Lana returned late in the afternoon, she seemed very disappointed that her father had left without her.

I spent the afternoon at Kenneth's.

"What was the happiest time in your life?" I asked him after making conversation for a quarter of an hour.

"When I was at my grandmother's place when I was small," he answered. "Riding horses and all that. Went hunting with my uncle."

Kenneth's maternal grandmother died last spring. He seemed very attached to her and told me about her death the first time I met him. His second most happy experience was his first year in boarding school; he was in the first grade. He could give me no example of the saddest time in his life. If he were granted three wishes, they would be: (1) "owning a horse, raising horses" (a surprisingly immediate response), (2) "raising a family," (3) "serving in the army."

I then asked him to tell me any story he would like.

"This is a story I remember," he said after a pause of more than five minutes. "We were small kids, me and my brother Albert. We was herding sheep. He went back from where I was herding. He never made it. He got lost. We had to look for him. Had to send for the police. A lot of people help. They found him at midnight."

"Tell me another story!" I asked when he had finished.

"When I stayed at Big Bead's ranch. I stayed there

three weeks taking care of the cattle." He stopped.

"When was that?" I asked finally.

"About two years ago."

"Where was it?"

"Around Mines. I was alone then. They just come up once a week. Every Friday."

"Were there any sheep there?"

"No, just horses and cattle."

"Did you like being alone?"

"Yes."

Every time I have seen Kenneth, he has been alone in his hogan. He always seems to be lying on his bed toying with something. Today it was a safety razor. Girlie magazines were scattered over the bed.

I asked him about boarding school in Utah and learned that there are between two and four students in a room and that the proctors are Hopi, Navaho, and Cherokee. The boys are kept pretty much away from girls, but sometimes get a chance to make love. "Then they go steady." None of the boys ever masturbate together; they do it alone. The teachers don't want them to, and if they are caught twice they are sent home. Kenneth doesn't see anything wrong with masturbation.

Kenneth does not dream much, but when he was little he did dream about *yeibechai*. "During the winter, there is a *yeibechai* ceremony. They go around and spank little kids. Then I dreamt about them. The second time they come around they bring candy. The *yeibechai* chased me around in the dream and tried to catch me. You have to be outside, but I went into somebody's place. They can catch you if you go out. I went into a hogan. There was somebody there but I can't remember who. Then I woke up." I was impressed by the way information concerning the ceremony was blended with the dream narration; no effort was made to differentiate verbally the two levels of reality. Kenneth's other dreams "are usually about horses —riding around and having one."

AUGUST 7

I ATTENDED A HOPI HUNTER'S DANCE and got talking to one man about "Navvies," whom he doesn't like. He claimed to have gone to school with Forster and then told me that Forster had been "fixed" a few years ago at the hospital "because he had too many kids." His wife —the one he never talks about—made him do it. "Then she ups and leaves him. She's still around. Well, that's Navvies for you."

AUGUST 8

I SPENT THE DAY VISITING the principals of the local schools. I was told that Harry Young was one of the slowest children in the school. He is an absentee problem. He learns something well one day and the next he acts as though he had never heard of it. He has a very low retention rate and is moody. His grades have declined dramatically in the last year.

Harold Kennedy stopped by tonight and told Forster that he had seen Sally at the Squaw Dance. She was over the hill with a lot of men.

AUGUST 9

Without mentioning her name, Forster told me at breakfast that his fourth wife had once had one hundred eighty dollars stolen from her in Phoenix. Forster had had to go to a friend, a white man who had lived on the reservation for many years, to borrow money to get back. Sometime later, when they were on vacation in Albuquerque, she had left a wallet containing two hundred eighty dollars in a store, but they had kept it for her.

Forster took the children to town to register for school.

As the fifteenth of August approaches, times goes slower and slower. It is very hard for me to go out and visit people and know at the same time that I am leaving. Most of my best informants have left Little Bluff anyway—for Utah to work as pickers, for mountain sheep camps, for Carteret. Forster isn't around much any more. He comes back every day from work tired and uncommunicative. Perhaps I spent too much time with him. Now that life at his place has more or less returned to normal—the kids registered for school today—I realize how exceptional all the activity in July, Forster's vacation, had been.

Much of my time now is spent in filling in details— short visits here and there. The frustration such visits bring when I discover my informants gone! I've finally started taking pictures, but it isn't much good. The Navaho insist upon dressing and posing. Candid shots are impossible.

All of this fill-in work has put me in a strange, nostalgic

sort of mood. I'm beginning to feel the burden of what I haven't accomplished—and there is so much. One thing bothers me more than I expected: the lack of contact with Forster's children. The only evidence of friendship I've had from them was Martha's silently handing me her brother's letter. She is now away at camp for a week. I've hardly noticed her absence. John is still resentful. Lana is too busy "running around," as Forster puts it, to get to know and Cora remains dully sunk in herself.

Then there is Forster—I suppose this disturbs me more than anything else—the conversation with the Hopi about Forster being sterilized a few years ago. From what I could gather, his wife—the one he has never really mentioned to me—forced him into it and then left him. I don't know if it is true, and there is no way of finding out —the Hopi didn't like the Navaho and used it as an example of their ugliness—but it would explain a lot. I really like Forster, and the whole affair depresses me tremendously.

As I was writing, Joan Shepard came into my hogan without knocking to borrow a dollar. Lana was waiting outside. Joan did not seem in the least embarrassed that I was half naked. She turned to the wall and waited for me to dress.

Tonight I made spaghetti. What a fiasco! I had promised Forster to make the "long noodles with chili" his sergeant friend from Brooklyn had made for him. The sauce turned out all right, but the spaghetti was just a soggy mess. I had forgotten to compensate for altitude—we are over four thousand feet high here—and I made enough for an army. Four pounds for five people. Everyone was very polite and assured me it was delicious, but at the end Forster suggested an easier way—canned spaghetti.

After dinner as I was asking Forster about his school experiences—he was spanked several times and even ran away once—a man from the finance company stopped by. He was a stranger and clearly didn't know the Navaho. He shouted at Forster and told him he'd better pay up. Forster had just paid the July installment, and it was already August. He couldn't go on running a month behind.

"I pay you next week," Forster said.

"No, you pay today, payday," the man ordered.

I could see Lana and John watching from the kitchen window.

"I'm expecting some money next week," Forster insisted dully.

"You've got money today, haven't you?" the white man asked.

"No, it all gone," Forster answered.

"All gone!"

"Yes, all gone. Vacation cost a lot of money."

It was finally agreed that Forster would send in fifty-four dollars next week.

After the man had gone, we painted the wagon wheels red with spray paint Forster had bought, and then John and Lana asked me to drive them to town, where they treated me to a coke float. Since they were all covered with paint, they were too embarrassed to get out of the car to buy the ice cream drinks and called a friend over instead. He couldn't get the order straight and kept saying "float coke," which Forster's children found hysterical.

As we were drinking the floats, Lana and John—half in English, half in Navaho—talked about the bill collector's visit. Lana asked her brother in English—she clearly wanted me to understand—whether the money Forster had borrowed was what he had given Sally. I could not understand John's answer in Navaho. Both of them seemed angry. From what I could gather, Forster intends to pay the finance company with their salaries next week.

AUGUST 10

FORSTER DID NOT GET HOME until well after eleven at night. One of the BIA drivers who is related to Forster by marriage is missing. He had gone out early this morning and did not come back at the expected time. He had seemed very depressed. His boss fears suicide. Forster, who had spent most of the evening looking for him unsuccessfully, seems very worried.

AUGUST 11

WILLY MURPHY IS AT HIS SISTER'S CAMP, Forster told me at breakfast. Big Singer is in a mountain camp near Frontier. He is at a Shooting Way but is not the medicine man. Forster asked around yesterday about the two men after I had told him that I hadn't been able to find them for several days. There are a number of points I want to check with them; I still do not know exactly why Willy moved to Little Bluff.

I spent most of the morning with Greg discussing the agricultural problems of the area. It appears that the irrigation system is not in use this year because there wasn't enough cooperation among the inhabitants of the area to clean it out. In previous years the BIA had organized the cleaning. Consider this with respect to the heterogeneous composition of Little Bluff; traditional patterns of cooperation, which run along clan and family lines, cannot function here.

Greg is planning to take a sweat bath tomorrow and has invited me to join him.

Forster returned from work disgusted with his missing relative. The man's car had broken down on an isolated dirt road, and rather than follow the road for help he had walked cross-country and didn't make it to a trading post until early this morning.

We all went to see a movie, *Wild on the Beach*. Forster and the children found it rotten.

AUGUST 12

FORSTER AND JOHN seemed very amused that I was going to take a sweat bath.

I arrived at Greg's place at nine. He was swimming in a muddy pool behind his house with a lot of children, who dived in and dog-paddled back to shore again and again. Greg climbed out and sat down next to me. He began to gossip about Forster. First he told me Forster's secret Navaho name and then asked if he was still drinking a lot. "Forster sure likes the red stuff. He used to get drunk all the time."

Greg assured me Forster had been married four times. His fourth wife left him for another man. She was much younger than Forster, played him for what he was worth, and then ran off with a man her own age. "He sure likes young girls," Greg commented.

"Have you seen many queers?" he asked suddenly.

I told him I hadn't.

"Well, I've only met one. He's half Hopi, half Navaho. He lives with the Hopi."

Greg began to brag about his own drinking. He had been arrested several times but always managed to get out of it. Of all the Navahos I've met, he is the vainest, and he seems compelled to put on "high-school" airs in my presence.

At nine thirty we walked back to his house, where he changed. Two male German shepherds started to play with each other. Greg's eight-year-old daughter began to giggle and then told the dogs they couldn't do that. We hitched two mules to an old rickety wagon, which we loaded with large logs from a nearby woodpile, picked a few melons in a neighboring field, and then drove to the sweat bath.

The bathhouse, which was hidden behind a hill, was a little mud-covered hogan, big enough for two people only. Near it was a pile of rocks, over which we built a fire. Two older men and two young boys joined us. As we waited for the rocks to warm, we sat in the sun eating the not yet fully ripe melons. I tried to obtain more information about Forster's wives from Greg, but he had lost interest in the subject. I asked him if Forster had ever been in the hospital. He said he had, several times, but knew nothing about what had happened to him there.

When the rocks were hot, we placed them in the center of the hogan and covered the entrance with two or three old army blankets. All six of us stripped: the men completely and the boys to their skivvies. The men then tied their foreskins closed with ribbons—I was told it was bad luck to look at the glans—and when Greg noticed that I hesitated he laughed and asked me if I was circumcised. I nodded. "Just tie a ribbon on anyway," he said. "I've known a lot of circumcised men in the army. I don't know the reasons for it. We Navaho don't go in for it much."

First the two older men went into the hogan and stayed for about ten minutes. I was told that in the old days they would have sung special songs but that nobody bothered much now. When they came out, they rubbed themselves down with sand and sucked the juice from the melons, spitting out the pulp. Greg and I crawled in next and stayed about as long, massaging ourselves down all the time. Unlike the older men, we washed ourselves afterward the water, which Greg had brought over in pails. The boys followed us. Each of us entered the sweat bath three times. Shortly after the bath was over, Greg left for a Land Board meeting, and I walked to School House.

AUGUST 13

FORSTER AND THE GIRLS did not come home last night. John did not know where they were. The kitchen was left in a mess.

At ten thirty this morning, Forster returned and came directly into my hogan. He and the girls had gone for a ride and spent the night in the car in the mountains somewhere. They were going to Carteret now. The kids needed some clothes. For the first time, Forster asked me if I wanted anything. He seemed jittery and promised to bring back a bottle of rosé for me. Just before he left, he told me that Sally was at her father's, Dan Shepard's, and if she stopped by—he tried to be casual—I was to tell her

he wanted his money. The poor man seemed afraid of
meeting her. He hardly stayed fifteen minutes.

AUGUST 14

FORSTER HAD DRIVEN TO Carteret again for
no particular reason. He seemed surprised that I enjoyed
the sweat bath and disappointed that there had been no
singing. Breakfast lasted for well over an hour. On the
back of a Cheerios box were pictures of North American
animals, which started Forster talking about his hunting
trips. I had already heard most of the stories. He brought
out a second box of cereal, which had pictures of Austra-
lian animals; he knew very little about them and seemed
uninterested in what I had to say about them. John was
very curious. I brought in a copy of Lloyd Warner's *A
Black Civilization,* which had pictures of aboriginals.
"They look just like Negroes," was Forster's only comment, although he looked with considerable fascination at
the pictures of their implements. Shortly after breakfast
the family left for Forster's sister's camp.

I stopped at Colin Curtis's twice today to say good-bye.
He was not in. Finally I left two dolls for his children
with a note.

Kenneth was asleep when I arrived at one this afternoon. His oldest brother, Tim, whom I had never met,
was sitting under a brush arbor. He complained of a stomach ache which he attributed first to having eaten too
many cookies in Carteret yesterday and then to the beer
party he had been to last night.

Unlike Kenneth, Tim is quick and talkative. He

seemed very much at ease with me and had no need to promote himself as his brother Albert, whom I met at the Shooting Way, had. He was learning welding at a vocational training college in Oakland, where he shares an apartment with a Sioux classmate. He is a Mormon but doesn't go to church. He would like to learn to play the guitar like his brother Albert, who plays with a Navaho rock band. Once they toured Oklahoma. Tim then gave me a detailed description of several mass murders. I was amazed at how much he knew about them. Then he told me about some Siamese twins, who were born with four legs and arms. He showed me their pictures, which were in the *National Enquirer*. On the subject of Squaw Dances, Tim talked only about the fights. "Only the young people like to fight—not the old ones. They like to show off. My brother Albert was slashed across the face with a razor last New Year's. . . ."

On the way to town, a pickup truck passed me with Dan Shepard, his daughter Joan, Helen, and another girl whom I had never seen before. One lock of her black hair was bleached blond. She waved. It must have been Sally.

Forster and the children returned in time for a community-center dance and then sat up until three in the morning drinking and singing Squaw Dance sway songs. At one time they all piled into the car and disappeared for an hour.

AUGUST 15

FORSTER ANNOUNCED THIS MORNING that he was not going to work. He did not feel well. He looked very hung-over. I drove to town to leave a message with his boss, and when I returned he was dressed and ready to go. The kitchen was filled with girls. Lana, who had not returned from the dance last night, had come back this morning with two friends, Betty and Anne. Forster was in his glory. He was taking them to Carteret for lunch. He introduced me to Anne two or three times, trying to feel her up each time, and then told both girls to talk to me "because I was real intelligent, and they should learn from me."

"Is he always like this?" Anne asked.

I shrugged.

"We watched him get stoned last night," Betty added, "so that we could get the car and drive around. We went up to see the fire. You know that big barn burned down. He passed out in the back seat and didn't see a thing." Both girls laughed.

Martha and Cora prepared a big breakfast with bacon and eggs in honor of my departure. Just as we were about to begin, Forster's mother-in-law, Hannah Cody, walked in. She had been living in a tent across the road for the past few days, weeding her fields. Forster immediately invited her to breakfast and offered her the only chair in the room. The rest of us had been standing around the table. Hannah sat down in her long gold dress and looked, not without a sign of disapproval, at her middle-aged son-in-law surrounded by six teen-age girls in shorts and slacks.

After breakfast I went to my hogan to pack and was joined by John and a friend, who had come to chat. John's friend was talkative and complained about his high-school principal, who wouldn't let the boys grow their hair long but would let the girls come to school in tight slacks. He asked me a lot of questions about New

York and my girl friends. John listened, curious, but never said a word.

Forster came in to tell me he was going to town for a few minutes but would be back in time to say good-bye. He never returned. Later in the day, from Gene's car, I saw Forster enter a supermarket in Carteret with Martha and Cora. The light turned green before I had a chance to call to him.

A NOTE ON THE
ORIGIN LEGEND OF ENEMY WAY

EACH OF THE NAVAHO CEREMONIALS, which, generally speaking, are designed to re-establish harmony between a man (the patient) and the universe, has what has been called an origin legend. These legends, whose component themes recur again and again, are not simply keys to the ceremonial activities but, as Joseph Campbell points out in *The Hero with a Thousand Faces,* they parallel on a mythic plane what occurs on a ritual level within the ceremonial itself. They are reflections of the basic ritual cycle of separation, initiation, and return expressed in terms of the adventures of a hero.

A hero ventures forth from the world of common day into a region of supernatural wonder: fabulous forces are there encountered and a decisive victory is won; the hero comes back from this mysterious adventure with the power to bestow boons on his fellow man.*

* Joseph Campbell, *The Hero with a Thousand Faces* (New York: Meridian Books, 1956), p. 30.

Not only do the legends parallel symbolically the ceremonial cycle in which, to take the case of Enemy Way, the patient is prepared to enter the sacred realm where, identified with the hero Monster Slayer, he kills the enemy ghost, and then returns to his everyday world a renewed man, but they also parallel the path the medicine man himself pursues as he learns the ceremony.*

The two versions of the Enemy Way legend told to me by Harold Kennedy and Colin Curtis and recorded in this book are confused and very incomplete. They both refer to the adventures of the Hero Twins—a legend which occurs with some variation in both the Navaho creation myth and in other origin legends and which is known as Monster Way. Little reference was made to the second part of the origin legend for Enemy Way—the War on Taos.

In order to clarify the material presented in this journal and to contrast it with a more complete version, I have made a summary of Monster Way, as it was recorded by Father Berard Haile, a Franciscan who lived on the reservation during the first part of this century.† Father Berard's informant did not believe that Monster Slayer himself ever had Enemy Way sung over him. Rather, he reported, it was Young Man of Jarring Mountain, who appears in the War on Taos, who was the first Enemy Way patient. Other Navahos, however, do believe that Monster Slayer was, in fact, the first patient. At any rate, he is regarded by everybody as a pattern for the ceremonial.

* Mary C. Wheelwright (recorder), *Navaho Creation Myth* (Santa Fe: Museum of Navajo Ceremonial Art, 1942), p. 17.
† Father Berard Haile, "Origin Legend of the Navaho Enemy Way," *Yale University Publications in Anthropology*, 17 (1938), pp. 9–319.

In the beginning, the legend starts without further explanation, conditions had become so terrible because of the women that the People moved from the lower to the upper world and agreed to live together in peace, but the women had not forgotten their evil ways and required the vigilance of the men. Four chiefs were appointed to watch over the young women and to see that they obtained husbands in the proper way, but each of the chiefs' own daughters managed to evade her father's eye. One abused herself with an elkhorn, the second with a quill, the third with a smooth stone stuck into the thick part of a leg sinew, and the fourth with a whittled-down sour cactus. Each girl conceived and gave birth to monsters—the Horned Monster, the Monster Eagle, Tracking Bear, and the Monsters That Kill with Their Eyes—which were carried away by the wind to the safety of the mountaintops. The son of the first chief was so enraged that he demanded his father's place as guardian, but his daughter, too, eluded him. She picked up a river stone and carried it with her as she walked in the direction of the rising sun.

There she had defecated, it seems, and had wiped her excrement with it. She had inserted the warm stone into her genitals, and, probably, was in her periods when she did this. Raising up her skirt she looked at her parts, and about that time the sun rose which, as it struck her vagina, sent a thrill through her.

She too conceived and gave birth to Lonely Traveling Big Yei. The monsters grew and began to devour all of the people without mercy.

Meanwhile Talking God came to First Man and First

Woman, who lived at Huerfano Mountain, and asked them what was under the dark cloud he had seen at the top of Gobernador Knob. At first, First Man showed no interest in the question, but encouraged by his wife, he finally climbed with much difficulty to the top of the peak.

He reached the spot where the dark cloud lay, sun's ray hung over it, rainbow hung over it, he found, a fine spray was drizzling. It certainly was a most beautiful spot. As though someone had smoothed out the sand, thus he found the place. And here he had come upon a babe, whose eyes were similar to charcoal, with not a speck of dirt on them.

Talking God was there, too. The two debated over who would take charge of the baby girl, and it was finally decided that First Man would have the child, because he could feed her with pollen, game broth, and the dew of beautiful flowers. Talking God would take her when she became a woman.

First Woman took care of the child for her husband, and called her "a woman she becomes time and again," or Changing Woman. Changing Woman grew very rapidly. Every four days she grew, and soon she was a woman.

First Man and First Woman hoped for a new generation to replace all the people who had been devoured by the monsters, and they instructed Changing Woman to tell them when her first flow came. They were scheming for a way in which the monsters could be overcome. Since Lonely Traveling Big Yei was the son of the Sun, he and the other monsters could be overcome only by weapons in the Sun's possession: the zigzag lightning arrow, the straight arrow, the sunray arrow, and the rainbow arrow, as well as the dark flint club, the blue flint club, the yellow flint club, and the serrated flint club.

When Changing Woman had her first period, First Man and First Woman arranged for a ceremony to be attended by the inner forms, or spirits, of all things. Changing Woman was made to run in the direction of the rising Sun and back, and as she ran she learned from the Sun that he himself had named her White Bead Woman. First Woman was pleased with this and dressed Changing Woman in white beads. When Changing Woman's second period came, Talking God was called and again Changing Woman ran, this time for the benefit of the Moon. Her new name, White Bead Woman, was confirmed by the voice of a rainbow.

Changing Woman now grew restless. One day, as she was walking in some sunny place a strange man told her to lay out some boughs in a circle with an opening to the east and to lie within it. This she did, and spent a sleepless and expectant night. Toward dawn, she fell asleep and dreamed that a man had lain down at her side. In fact, it was the Sun who had caused her to think so. Still restless, she wandered to a place called Dripping Water, where she bathed herself completely and then lay down on her back, letting the water drip into her vagina. The light of the Moon shone on it, and she imagined that the same man slept with her. She soon showed signs of pregnancy, and after nine nights, gave birth to the twins Monster Slayer and Born for Water, who were moved by a sunray from mountaintop to mountaintop until they became men.

When the Twins were grown, First Man called them to him and told them to visit their father, the Sun, in order to obtain the weapons necessary for slaying the monsters. He warned them not to tell the Sun their purpose because the most ruthless of the monsters, Lonely Traveling Big Yei, was also his son. First Man crossed a pair of sunrays and a pair of rainbows under the Twins' feet, and they glided from mountaintop to mountaintop toward the Sun, stopping occasionally for visits. One of their stops was Spider's house.

"So it's you, my children. Your coming was reported!" Spider said to them.

"We are on a journey to our father, the Sun," the Twins said.

"Certainly your father has no pity," Spider told them. "Dawn Woman's daughter, Dawn Girl, is his wife. He has children. There are boys and girls who are your brothers and sisters. But in the absence of any other help, you may use this."

And he gave them each a pair of live plumes.

With the aid of the plumes, the Twins were able to surmount one obstacle after another—a rock cliff, needle cactus, a sand slide, cutting reeds which covered them with red blood spots—until they were stopped by a wide body of blue water. Not knowing what to do, the Twins walked along the water's edge until, suddenly, a thin old man called Field Rat approached them.

"Your project is quite difficult," he told them. "How do you expect to enter, my children? Your father has no mercy. The so-called Big Bear is his entrance guard. The Big Snake and Thunder and the Whirlwind are his entrance guards."

Field Rat then gave them the secret names of the guards.

The Twins continued along the water's edge, and again they were approached by a strange man, who gave them something which was tied up in fabric and which he said to use when their father offered them a smoke. And they walked on, wondering how they were going to cross the water, when still again they were approached, this time by

Holy Young Man, who was born in the interior of Glittering Mountain, and by Holy Boy. Holy Young Man and Holy Boy gave the Twins specially marked bows and arrows, which carried them across the water to the other shore. They came then to a blue house guarded by Big Bear, Big Snake, Thunder, and Whirlwind, but by uttering the names that Field Rat had told them they were able to pass unharmed.

When at last they came to the Sun's house, they were greeted by Dawn Girl, the Sun's wife, and by two of her children, who folded them up in a dawn curtain, a sky-blue curtain, a curtain of the evening twilight, and a curtain of darkness and hid them in safety. In the afternoon, the Sun returned and immediately asked about the black object he had seen. At first, Dawn Girl said nothing, but finally she answered that two who claimed to be the Sun's children had come. The Sun searched until he found them. He lassoed the Twins with zigzag lightning and dashed them down four times on jutting flint projections, but the boys were saved each time by the live plumes that Spider had given them. Then the Sun tried to plug them into holes, but again the live plumes saved them. And the Sun tried to burn them in an agate-fueled sweat house, but the Moon had dug a hole there and given them rocks with which to protect themselves.

"You ought to come into being," the Sun said finally. (The Twins were not fully formed at this time.) He called his children, Dawn Children, who rubbed the Twins with pollen, molded them in their own likeness, and dressed them as they themselves were dressed.

"There is still one trial left," the Sun announced. He offered them his pipe to smoke, and with the aid of the strange package the Twins were able to relish the smoke. Then the Sun recognized the Twins as his children and rubbed their feet with the remaining tobacco. He gave them food, but however much they ate, the bowl was always full.

"Why have you come to visit me, my children?" the Sun asked. He offered them many things—white beads, horse figures made of different stones, all kinds of game—but the Twins refused them all. At last they asked for the weapons with which they could destroy the monsters.

"That is out of the question!" the Sun answered. "What will you do with them?"

"We have already determined how we shall use them, my father," they answered. "Conditions are getting terrible. Lonely Traveling Big Yei has devoured us all! Horned Monster has devoured us all, and so have Monster Eagle and Monsters That Kill with Their Eyes."

The Sun bowed his head and held it in his hands.

"How great you are, my children!" he said at last. "You must not do it! He is your older brother. He is my son, this Big Yei."

But the Sun agreed to lend them the weapons on the condition that he himself would have the first shot.

"I shall never place the weapons in your hands altogether," the Sun said.

The Twins left with their father to find Lonely Traveling Big Yei. They stopped above Mount Taylor, where, looking for an excuse not to give them the weapons, the Sun asked them to identify a number of places.

"It is evident that you are in earnest!" he said when they had answered all of his questions correctly. "You are certainly great ones! He is your older brother. I have loved him above all others. Be sure not to bother him. I myself shall make the first move. Then I shall not regret it."

The Twins descended to Mount Taylor, where the Big

Yei lay. He threw flint clubs at them, but the Twins were able to duck out of the way. Their father attacked Lonely Traveling Big Yei with his lightning, removing his disks of agate, turquoise, and white bead and disarming him. Then the Twins killed the monster with the zigzag lightning arrow. They returned home to their mother, who did not recognize them at first.

Monster Slayer vanquished and took trophies from the monsters which had been devouring the people—Horned Monster, Monster Eagle, Monsters That Kill with Their Eyes, Tracking Bear, Big Gray Yei, and Traveling Stone. He spared only the Frog Peoples (who had been sinking people into bogs and water and who promised him to call for rain), the Big Toads, and the Syphilis People, who were the last resource of painful instruction.

When all of the monsters were destroyed, the Twins wrapped up their weapons in a rainbow and returned them to their father. In exchange, the Sun gave them a mountain mahogany stick on which he drew an imitation of zigzag lightning and straight lightning.

"Henceforth you shall make this alone," he said. "Never again shall anyone receive zigzag lightning in their hand."

The Twins, who were able to keep the sunray arrow and the sunray upon which they traveled, left for Water-Flows-Together.